Oladele Olatunde Layiwola
...teacher, mentor, idea

About the Series

The African Humanities Series is a partnership between the African Humanities Program (AHP) of the American Council of Learned Societies and academic publishers NISC (Pty) Ltd*. The Series covers topics in African histories, languages, literatures, philosophies, politics and cultures. Submissions are solicited from Fellows of the AHP, which is administered by the American Council of Learned Societies and financially supported by the Carnegie Corporation of New York.

The purpose of the AHP is to encourage and enable the production of new knowledge by Africans in the five countries designated by the Carnegie Corporation: Ghana, Nigeria, South Africa, Tanzania, and Uganda. AHP fellowships support one year's work free from teaching and other responsibilities to allow the Fellow to complete the project proposed. Eligibility for the fellowship in the five countries is by domicile, not nationality.

Book proposals are submitted to the AHP editorial board which manages the peer review process and selects manuscripts for publication by NISC. In some cases, the AHP board will commission a manuscript mentor to undertake substantive editing and to work with the author on refining the final manuscript.

The African Humanities Series aims to publish works of the highest quality that will foreground the best research being done by emerging scholars in the five Carnegie designated countries. The rigorous selection process before the fellowship award, as well as AHP editorial vetting of manuscripts, assures attention to quality. Books in the series are intended to speak to scholars in Africa as well as in other areas of the world.

The AHP is also committed to providing a copy of each publication in the series to university libraries in Africa.

*early titles in the series was published by Unisa Press, but the publishing rights to the entire series are now vested in NISC

Published in this series

...a story that must be told never forgives silence.
– Okey Ndibe

What the forest told me

Yoruba hunter, culture
and narrative performance

Ayo Adeduntan

AHP
Publications

NiSC

Originally published in 2014 by Unisa Press, South Africa
under ISBN: 978-1-86888-739-2

This edition published in South Africa on behalf of the African Humanities Program
by NISC (Pty) Ltd, PO Box 377, Grahamstown, 6140, South Africa
www.nisc.co.za

NISC first edition, first impression 2019

ISBN: 978-1-920033-41-5 (print)
ISBN: 978-1-920033-42-2 (PDF)
ISBN: 978-1-920033-43-9 (ePub)

Project Editor: Tshegofatso Sehlodimela
Book Designer: Kedibone Phiri
Editor: Gail Malcomson
Typesetting: Nozipho Noble
Indexer: Hannalie Knoetze

Contents

List of Plates & Tables

Acknowledgements

These acknowledgements, like all attempts at paying bad debts, are not a successful catalogue of all the individuals and institutions to whom I owe the final completion of this work; the limitation of human memory always moderates one's desire to write such a roll.

I am grateful to the American Council Learned Societies for the African Humanities Postdoctoral Fellowship award which allowed me the facilities needed to complete the manuscript for this book.

The immensity of Dele Layiwola's advisory and mentoring efforts transcends the immediate attainment of publishing a book. His presence is such that never leaves.

Sola Olorunyomi (Uncle Ẹ́ss; Bàmi) was a prime accessory to the beginning of this work as a PhD research. With precision of a sorcerer, he would 'intrude' whenever I was in dire need of a helping hand. He sometimes went to such extent as 'looting' his wife's kitchen to provision mine. His interventions in those blue moments were so numerous that it was only sensible to stop saying 'thank you'.

It was in a climate conducive to interrogation and rebellion, provided by the entire family of the Institute of African Studies, University of Ibadan, that this work began and came to fruition. Ohioma Pogoson was generous with encouragement and humour that made the most trying moments seem like trivia. The avuncular counsel and goodwill of O.B. Olaoba and P.B. Unuofin were invaluable. Isaac Olawale Albert, I.A. Jimoh, Aderonke Adesanya, Titus K. Adekunle, Wale Ajayi and Remi Aduradola nudged me when necessary.

Rotimi Babatunde is both a reliable friend and an entirely unwise creditor. In 2006, the processing of some of the data used in this work wrecked his computer. He also intervened materially at crucial moments. And Kunle Okesipe is neither wiser. He often yielded too easily to blackmail and would empty his pockets to give all or to prove that there was no salary yet. Those two are kindred spirits that have haunted me for close to two decades.

Friend and 'tormentor' from childhood, Honourable Tunde Ojo, put vehicle and personnel at my disposal during my trips to Oke-Ogun sites. As an informant, his cues were so numerous and equally so tempting that it was often difficult to choose final samples.

My mum, Bernice Aderoju, never really gave up on her restless and footloose son who, instead of working and 'settling down', went about with camera and voice recorder collecting weird and wild stories. My friend Folake Oladeji, and my sisters, Leye and Sade, generously forgave recurring stress-induced withdrawal and tantrums, and continued to show the needed love and support.

In my perennial search for information, the following family of friends never tired at pointing out where to get what and helping with last-minute clarification: Messrs Abiodun Fadiji (Ordinary), Dapo Odetunde (Akala), Ayodele Abiodun (Engineer), Femi Egbebowale (Omo Egbe), Adekunle Onifade (Sir K), Gbenga Kehinde (Ilora), Segun Taiwo (Sigo), E.B. Adumaradan (Ijesa) and Ademola Joseph (Yellow). I am grateful to the authorities of the Broadcasting Corporation of Oyo State (BCOS) for the permission granted me to observe live broadcasts and access recorded ones. Initially, Tope Salawu of BCOS facilitated my meeting with Mrs Dasola Akinlabi and Mr Lekan Babatunde, producers of Ọdẹ Akọni and Ọdẹtẹdó respectively. My debt to Kola Akintayo, Olabisi George Gbamolefa, and Yahya Lateef, who volunteered to be my informants in Oyo and Osun States without charge, is enormous. I am no less grateful to Mrs Akinlabi and Mr Babatunde for guidance and information. The hunters who provided me the data and insights are just too numerous to list.

My residency at the International Institute for the Advanced Studies of Cultures, Institutions and Economic Enterprise (IIAS) was invaluable. Irene K. Odotei, Emmanuel Ayeampong and Ato Quayson were pleasant hosts. In the last adjustment made to the script, the suggestions and counsels of Kwesi Yankah and Kofi Anyidoho were indispensable. Co-fellows at IIAS, Gbemisola Adeoti and Aaron Mushengezi, made my stay memorable.

Later, my wife, Jumoke, would affirm the work's quality in such strong terms that I was sometimes almost tempted to agree with her. She and my daughter, Jọláadé, were an indispensable company.

To all that I have tried and failed to recall, these acknowledgements are just an infinitesimal fragment of the huge eternal debt I owe all of you.

Preface

Studies of Yoruba culture and performance have focused predominantly on standardised performance forms, such as *ìjálá*, *èsà*, *ìyèrè* and *àló*, ignoring the more prevalent performance culture that has convolved with everyday human routine. The drama, poetry and narrative embedded in such practices as hawking, preaching and conversation have not received enough consideration. A related problem is the question of taxonomy. Existing studies have too frequently ignored the elastic nature of many African cultural sites. The resulting models of Yoruba performance are therefore either inadequate or outmoded as a result of exigent transformations and modification of the cultural practices.

Like the priest and the masked dancer, the Yoruba hunter is a primal actor in cultural production. More than the priest and the dancer, he detests boundaries and thrives on breaching them. His exploits therefore provide a consummate example of the slipperiness of assigning performance to categories. The hunter's performance challenges students of culture to stay alert, for his next performance may render their last definition invalid. This book uses narratives which tell of the Yoruba hunters' exploits to establish the relevance of performance to cultural sites that have previously been considered silent and banal. This assumed silence is especially pertinent in the case of the hunters' exploits because of a cultural and professional ethic that forbids them to tell their stories at home.

Despite this code of silence, Yoruba hunters' stories are told today and have even emerged as a popular form of television and radio entertainment. The outgrowth of the hunters' narratives in broadcast media exemplifies the dialectic of tradition and change in which contemporary practices necessitate a review and modification of norms.

The hunters' narratives also provide an index to the Yoruba understanding and explanation of their world, a cosmology that negates the anthropocentric view of creation. In a very literal sense, man, in this peculiar world, is an equal actor with animal and nature spirits with whom he constantly contests and negotiates space. Although this worldview has influenced the vision of such modern literary artists as D.O. Fagunwa and Amos Tutuola, the narratives that produced it have rarely been considered as art in their own right. A close individual appraisal of the texts and contexts of oral performance forms avoids the pitfalls of generalisation that characterise many attempts at describing the poetics of oral performance, and additionally yields insight into key aspects of Yoruba culture. This book is therefore an attempt to give the performative aspects of human activities the attention they merit. After all, it is these activities that the literary and verbal arts purport to mimic in the first place.

1

Hunter, Hunting and a Yoruba World

Introduction

Man has hunted animals for millions of years (Hill 1982). From being a mere means of subsistence, hunting has evolved into a cultural complex with different significance for different peoples. The table is just a starting point. In traditional Yoruba society, the hunters were the elite on whom society depended for its security and intelligence. To date, the same nominal *ọdẹ* denotes hunter and security guard. In many pre-colonial Yoruba societies, the hunters constituted a high percentage of the army. In areas without specific military designations, hunters were simply pressed into service any time the community was threatened by invasion. In his PhD thesis, Ogunsina (1987:142) writes: 'the Yoruba wars in the pre-colonial times . . . contributed to making the hunter prominent in the society'.

Even in the twentieth-century state, when many such wars are seen as communal clashes and therefore become illegitimate, hunters still function in a similar capacity. In communities like Tedé, Àgọ́-Àrẹ and Ṣakí, all in the Òkè-Ògùn area of Oyo State, the nomadic Bororo herdsmen occasionally graze their herds on farmlands during planting season. Any year that such an incursion is large enough to threaten the year's harvest, the hunters are called out to put the herdsmen to flight. In modern states like Côte d'Ivoire and Sierra Leone that have recently gone through wars, 'hunters,' writes Leach (2000:586), 'are being asked to play roles in defence *which reinvoke older forms of hunter warriordom* now joined to modern state interests' [my italics].

The contemporary hunter is also a security guard, the one who protects his society from the Other, the unknown and the unpleasant. In twentieth-century Côte d'Ivoire, the disappearance of wildlife and the rise of unemployment and its attendant criminality have combined to resituate the hunter as a significant social actor (Basset 2003). The hunters, renowned for their extraordinary ability to pacify the enemy, are currently being recruited as security guards by banks and other institutions. In Ibadan, one of the areas considered in this study, a similar situation has occurred. With robbers becoming more defiant of the law enforcement agents, the residents have not only lost confidence in the police, but have also come to view them with the same suspicion reserved for thieves and armed robbers. In the Òké-Àdó and Bẹẹrẹ areas of the city, the hunters' security services are in increasing demand from banks and hotels. Coordinated by Kọ́lá Akíntáyọ̀, himself a hunter, the hunters' guild in the area has registered itself with the appropriate authorities as a security firm, Ọdẹ Plus. Akíntáyọ̀ says:

> Nígbà t'ó di wípé àwọn ọlọ́sa ya bo gbogbo ìlú Ìbàdàn, àwọn ìlú wáá ké bá mi pé kíni mo le se láti ran àwọn lọ́wọ́. Mo ní t'ééyàn bà fi irú àwọn ọdẹ tí ń p'erin tí ń p'ẹfọ̀n yìí sọ́ àdúgbo, ọkàn ó balẹ̀ ẹ. Mo wá lọ register Ọdẹ Plus.

> [One time when robbers besieged the entire Ibadan city, people ran to me for help. I then thought that if one could make use of the hunters that kill elephants and buffaloes as security men, there would be peace. So I went on and got *Ọdẹ Plus* registered.][1]

As an adept at 'braving dangers of the great animals of the bush and the supernatural powers that would thwart him' (Herskovits and Herskovits 1958:29), the hunter has also been assigned the related role of founder and a scout. Olomola (1990:26) notes:

> Famous traditions were built around notable hunters in various traditions of origin and in histories of the growth and development of various states and kingdoms of the Yoruba. The stories of origin generally depict hunters as aboriginal settlers and often as scouts and pathfinders who led the first settler-groups to the traditional homeland.

The origin narratives of such Yoruba towns and cities as Ògbómọ̀ṣó, Ẹdẹ and Òṣogbo are ready examples. Specifically, the Ògbómọ̀ṣó narrative, entitled *Ogbori Elemoso* by Lérè Pàímọ́, has been performed in the last three decades as a TV drama, stage play and home video.

The hunter's special role derives in large part from his relationship to the extra-mundane. To the Yoruba, the bush or forest is not just the habitat of flora and fauna, but also of spirits – *iwin, ẹbọra, ànjọ̀ọ̀nú, sẹrankosènìyàn, ọ̀rọ̀*, and so on. In other words, the bush or forest is a realm of the infinite where the giant rat may tie up the hunter's dog, the ìrókò (a tree, the *Chlorophora excelsa*) might tell the hunter in which direction to seek game, and porcupines could perform in a concert. Literary critic Cooper (1998:40) describes this reality as 'an intricate and indivisible mosaic of the universe' which 'contests the divide between the human and the divine, the animate and inanimate, objects and humans'. Apter (1992:175) also notes:

> [The] bush is the place of ghosts, demons, monsters, even inverted societies which only the most powerful hunters and heroes can survive. It is also the habitat of dangerous animals and special plants used by herbalists to make

juju medicines. In ritual, the bush shrine is off-limit to the uninvited and uninitiated. It is the domain of powers which dwell in ponds, streams, hills and trees, but which roam freely and capriciously. The bush is wild, dangerous, uncultivated – it intrudes on farms and has to be cut back. In a deeper sense, it represents the void, the unknown, the other side of social life – bad death, estrangement, unbound space, unpredictability, chaos.

As a habitué of this realm that forecloses finitude, the hunter is in the vanguard of his society's eternal quest to domesticate the unknown.

The Yoruba suppose that the hunter has been part of their world since the primordial time. In Òsá Méjì, an odù of Ifá, a divination system considered by the Yoruba to be of primordial origin, the personifications of Earth and Heaven (Àjàláyé and Àjàlórun, respectively) are cast as hunters (Abimbola 1969a). These two friends both agree to hunt in a particular bush. The expedition is unsuccessful as their only kill is a palm-sized rodent. Neither of the two friends would cede the game to the other, and in the ensuing conflict, virtually the entire earthly creation suffers adversity: drought, flood, fire, barrenness, mortality, and so on. Only a sacrifice voluntarily officiated by the vulture re-establishes the umbilical between Earth and Heaven, restoring peace and stability. In another narrative variously performed as ìjálá (poetry as performed by hunters) or ìyèrè (poetry as performed by babaláwo, the Ifá priests), Heaven the hunter is Gbùélè or Olúgbúèlè (Yemitan 1963) or Gbúèdé (Abimbola 1969a), and Earth the hunter is Wawa (Yemitan 1963) or Waawaa (Abimbola 1969a). In the ìjálá version, relations between the two friends break down when Earth betrays Heaven, resulting in similar afflictions to those described in Òsá Méjì. On the instruction of Olódùmarè, Òrúnmìlà, the primordial babaláwo and personification of Ifá, later brokers peace and normalcy is restored. At the core of all of these narratives is the portrait of the hunter as an indivisible complex of the mundane (Earth) and the supernatural (Heaven), a cosmic system that ruptures the moment the two become isolated.

As the third eye that sees through the opaque screen between the self and the mysterious Other, the hunter – a scout and pathfinder – helps the community to access the unknown. At the end of the sixteenth century when Ògbólú, the Aláàfin of Òyó, and a section of his council broached the possibility of relocating the capital of the empire from Ìgbòho back to Katunga (the initial site), many people, among them members of the council, were opposed to it. In the bid to thwart the plan, those in opposition contrived to use men masked as ghosts to scare off the emissaries sent by the Aláàfin to survey Katunga. Troubled by the failure of the advance party, the Aláàfin sent six notable hunters to reconnoitre the 'ghost-occupied' Katunga. The hunters not only unmasked the 'ghosts,' but also brought them to the capital in fetters (Adedeji 1981; Smith 1988). Even given that the men were not ghosts after all, the choice of hunters as scouts in the narrative nevertheless highlights their role as agents of demystification.

One implication of the danger that the bush poses to the hunter is that he, as a matter of course, has to rig himself out with medicine and magical powers. Agbájé (1989:114) describes this necessity:

> *Yàtò sí pé àwọn odẹ a máa ṣe òògùn àwúre ẹran pípa, wọn tún maa ńlo oríṣìríṣìí agbára tí wọn bá fẹ́ lo pa eranko abìjà. Wọn maa ńlo áwọn òògun bí àfẹ́ẹ̀rí, egbé ati ọfọ̀. Tí egbé bá gbé odẹ kúrò níbi tí òhun àti eranko bá gbé wọn [sic] ìjàkadì, yóó tún ìbon rè kì kí ó tún [tó] máa to eran náà lọ láti yìn ín níbon lẹ́ẹ̀kejì.*

[Apart from their use of luck charms that guarantee them good kills, the hunters also employ all sorts of magical powers to confront malevolent animals. They use such powers as charms that make them invisible, make them disappear from somewhere and appear elsewhere, and incantation. When the hunter thus disappears from the place where he has been locked in a fight with the animal, the respite allows him to reload his gun before he confronts the animal once more to fire at it.]

The above is just one example of the necessity of the hunter's knowledge of supernatural powers. Cases abound of hunters trading one favour or another for medicine, charms or some other power with spirits. Invariably, the hunter is then regarded as a sort of repository of herbal and magical powers and knowledge. As Ògúndélé Ògúndèjì of Òjé-Owódé, a veteran hunter and guard, said to me, 'tí odẹ bá di òġbólògbó odẹ, àgbà ìsègùn ní í dà' [when the hunter gets very old, he evolves into an experienced medicine man].[2] The hunter often therefore finds himself playing the role of a healer. In fact, there are examples of hunters who have retired to full-time herbal medicine and healing practice. Narratives of their hunting days are their credentials.

Ìgbẹ́ Alágogo: A glimpse into the hunters' world

Ìgbẹ́ Alágogo, a seasonal hunting expedition in Òjé-Owódé, Oyo State, is a living illustration of the hunter's place in the Yoruba world. In some parts of the Òkè-Ògùn area, the communal hunting expedition used to be a regular yearly exercise, in which hunters and non-hunters voluntarily participated. It was part of the school calendar in secondary schools in such rural communities as Tedé, Àgọ́-Àrẹ and Àgọ́-Àmọ́dù until the 1990s. On the appointed day, interested teachers and students with some hunting experience led others into the bush some distance away from the school, ferreting out animals and hounding them with dogs. An originary type of this practice, of which the secondary school variant is evidently an outgrowth, still exists in Òjẹ́-Owódé, a community in the area. At the time of the fieldwork on which the study is based (2005–2010), no other known community in the study areas had either planned on or conducted such a communal expedition in about seven years, although Okebalama (1991) has written on a similar practice among the Ubakala Igbo of Imo State in Nigeria. In Òjẹ́-Owódé, the expedition had been suspended for about two years due to the death of the Ọlọ́jẹ̀ẹ́, the *ọba* of the town (many cultural activities are held in abeyance when this position, a high priest of sorts, is vacant). It only resumed in 2006, after a new Ọlọ́jẹ̀ẹ́ was installed.

Ìgbé Alágogo takes place during the dry season – when there is little or no work on the farm – and it goes on for about three months with breaks on Friday and Sunday to allow the Christian and Muslim participants to worship. Every night save Thursday and Saturday a boy makes the round sounding a gong all over the community (see Plate 1.1). The boy is among the family of the *Alágogo*, that is, a kind of prefect among the non-hunters. People call out to the boy from everywhere, '*Ìgbẹ̀ e'bo?*' [Which forest/bush?] and he responds, '*Igbó Ọba Sẹ̀kẹ̀rẹ̀*' [the Forest of Ọba Sẹ̀kẹ̀rẹ̀] or any other zone that the older *Alágogo* himself has marked for expedition the next day.

Plate 1.1: The *Alágogo* boy (left) and his friends making a night round

Plate 1.2: Participants converge as a family arrives on a motorbike

From the *Alágogo* boy's end of the exchange, there are multiple signifieds. First, he identifies a place, namely the bush in which hunting would take place. Other unstated signifieds include the time and place of the rendezvous. The distance of a forest or bush determines the time that participants should converge at the usual place. For Ọba Sẹ̀kẹ̀rẹ̀ mentioned above, for example, people begin to converge from 11:00 for an expedition beginning around noon (see Plate 1.2).

The people read all the details in the boy's phrasal response. His response – and this is very important – also indicates a warning that farmers and hunters who have traps laid out in the identified area should remove them early the next day. It is arguably to allow time to remove the traps that the expedition does not always begin before noon. Any trap not removed may be legitimately confiscated by anyone who sees it; should a person or dog be injured by a trap, the owner is subject to a fine. Like an active minefield, the bush must be defused in order that non-hunters might tread it safely.

The *Alágogo*'s role is to supervise the movement and activities of the non-professional hunters in the expedition. He has some experience in reading the direction of the hunters' movement through the occasional reports of their guns. As non-hunter participants in the expedition arrive, gun-toting hunters also arrive but do not converge with the non-hunters. They simply go on with their hunting. When all the hunters are out of sight, the *Alágogo* summons all the participants and gives his blessing (see Plate 1.3).

Plate 1.3: The *Alágogo* gives his blessing and declares the day's expedition open

He, in addition, warns them: '*Ẹ má saájú àwọn ọlọ́dẹ o*' [Please, don't go ahead of the hunters]. As the non-hunters' guide, the *Alágogo* in turn depends on the hunters for guidance. A liminal figure in his own right, the *Alágogo* reads what the faint gunshots imply about the direction of the hunters' movement and sounds out his gong in a sort of translation. His reading of the gunshots demands its own special expertise, as echoes from the surrounding rocks could easily lead a non-hunter, or a less skilled *Alágogo*, in the wrong direction. The hunters constitute the avant-garde here in the most literal sense. In the Ọ̀jẹ́-Owódé expedition, the hunters often put about twice the distance from the *Alágogo* as the *Alágogo* puts between himself and the non-hunters, thereby doubling the guarantee that no person strays into the turf not yet covered by the hunters' vanguard.

The *Alágogo*'s primary role is that of guide to the non-hunters, but he also adjudicates. He settles cases relating to the confiscation of traps and accidents. More significantly, he impounds any game disputed by the non-hunters, taking it for his own. But the hunters too are human, and in the event of multiple hits, argument over whose shot felled the animal sometimes creates animosity, even between friends. The jurisdiction of the *Alágogo*, however, does not stretch into the hunters' space. The hunters design their own system of adjudication presided over by the *àgbà ọdẹ* (old hunters). Special care is, in fact, taken not to let a non-hunter in.

In the *Ìgbẹ́ Alágogo* expedition, as in other hunting situations, the hunter uses a social cordon to insulate himself from the non-hunters. This isolation mirrors the hunter's attitude to his narratives. His world and its reality, in a manner of speaking, proscribe narrativity. Paradoxically, this attitude seems like the obverse of a role identified earlier, namely: the hunter as the third eye of his community. The hunter is familiar with the bush and a witness to its infinite weird possibilities, but some ethic forbids him to give total narrative expression to his experience. The *Alágogo*'s role, in some ways, is to ensure that man does not stray into the realm of the weird until it has been explored and tamed by the hunter/pacifier.

Nevertheless, the hunter's story is told. The ethic of such total silence is only manageable in a culture that is innocent of storytelling altogether. White's (1996:274) observation is instructive in this regard:

> So natural is the impulse to narrate, so inevitable is the form of narrative for any report of the way things really happened, that narrativity could appear problematical only in a culture in which it was absent.

As such, narrativity is a prime condition of human communication. Barthes (1996:46) agrees that 'under . . . almost infinite diversity of forms, narrative is present in every age, in every place, in every society . . . narrative is international, transhistorical, transcultural: it is simply there like life itself'. The hunter's narrative is, in this manner, mediated between the urge to tell stories and cultural ethic of discreetness.

Folklore and redefinition of performance

It is a fair observation that modern African writing is, at least by half, an offspring of traditional verbal art and performance. This view becomes more problematic, however, when the traditional verbal form is seen as a slough that the modern literary form has cast off, leaving the former in the museum to be marvelled at as curio. For example, in Nigeria, new forms such as stand-up comedy and float advertisements are now established performances, yet the performative practices from which they emerged, such as conversational jokes and open market touting, are still alive. The hunter's narrative, a form that has influenced not only D.O. Fagunwa and Amos Tutuola but also, to some extent, Wole Soyinka and Ben Okri, is another obvious example. This art form is not only alive but also finding new audience in the broadcast media.

As early as the 1970s, the ethnography of speaking school of ethnology pioneered by Dell Hymes called attention to the need to focus on the artistic quality of some forms of human communication to which our perception, trained to see only normative forms, has blinded us. Similarly, Yerkovich (1983:279) notes:

> Careful observation as well as extensive audio recording of conversational interaction is necessary for us to discover and analyse the narrative forms of folklore which are products of our everyday discourse. Still we have only begun to explore the possibilities for analysis which the social situation provides. We have yet to deal at length with the parts of that conversational process *which are artistic in their own right* [my italics].

On the African side of the Atlantic, some researchers have attempted to examine this area of culture and performance. Oyegoke (1994), Oha (1998), and Young (2004) have examined testimony in the church, modern 'mythmaking' and confession at truth and reconciliation commissions, respectively, as forms of performance.

A closely related idea from the folklore approach is a more expansive definition of performance. The orthodox conception of the term invokes the modern theatre or the communal arena where easily identifiable forms like drama and dance are performed. Bauman (1973:13) has argued that since traditional formal performance largely imitates reality, there is also a need to engage the reality that it deals with in the very process of its unfolding:

> Thus conceived, performance is a mode of language use, a way of speaking. The implication of such a concept for a theory of verbal art is this: it is no longer necessary to begin with artful texts, identified on independent formal grounds and then reinjected into situations of use, in order to conceptualise verbal art in communicative terms. Rather . . . performance becomes constitutive of the domain of verbal art as spoken communication.

The Yoruba culture is replete with such performative communication: ìpolówó poetry [hawker's advertisement] (Osundare 1991), curses and prayer in churches, political rallies and campaigns (Schechner 1993), and informal radio programmes. Beyond identifying these forms, it is necessary to examine their performativity.

In much the same way that postcolonial attempts at challenging the Western grand narrative sometimes read into African culture and worldview categories that unrepresentatively mimic the Western model, we sometimes conceive of traditional arts and culture as analogues of some Western forms. Though such classification purports to enhance ease of recognition for students from other cultural backgrounds, the peculiar colour of the artistic form under study is often lost in a foreign gloss. Much scholarly energy has been dissipated in attempting to prove that, like the West, Africa has epic (Okpewho 1979), theatre (Echeruo 1973; Rotimi 1981), long narrative equivalents to prose (Chinweizu, Jemie and Madubuike 1980; Roscoe 1971), and so on, forgetting that one culture's art does not necessarily need to mimic another's to also qualify as art. Though scholarship in culture and performance seems to have gradually overcome much of the reductionism, there remains a tendency to concentrate on only the standardised forms like àló, ìtàn, ìjálá, and so on (see, for example, Abimbola 1969b). Marginal forms, such as conversational narratives, dialogues, jokes and dramatic performances that defy, even in indigenous terms, such neat naming and classification abound.

The task of describing the norms and standards of cultural behaviours sometimes blinds us to some level of licence tolerable in the very culture under study. The Yoruba culture, like many other primarily oral cultures, is of such elasticity that aberrant and new entries often settle in for good. Admittedly, such new developments may sometimes die away in the face of conservative opposition, but there are also many instances of successful perpetuation of the new. For example, the ìjálá of Àlàbí Ògúndépò upsets some of the traditional norms identified by Babalola (1966). Ògúndépò has created a complex musical accompaniment for the performance which, unlike in the classical call-and-response type performed by Ògúndáre Fóyánmu, it is difficult for the audience to participate in. For Ògúndépò, this modification is not necessarily aimed at banishing the audience to the sidelines, but is an attempt to professionalise the art.[3] Many performances of Ifáyẹmí Ẹlẹ́buìbọ́n, a *babaláwo*, negate some aspects of the model of ìyèrè (performance of poetry by the *Ifá* priests) described by Olatunji (1972:85) as 'only chanted on ritual occasions', and a form in which 'no room is left for the chanter to be creative'. The album *Ayé Di Jágbà-n-Rúdu* by Ẹlẹ́buìbọ́n is just one example of his many attempts at appropriating the sacred form to critique the social and political hegemonies. The study therefore looks at the hunters' narratives with consideration for such elements, old and new, that are distinct from the known order.

Scope and methodology

The study was conducted between 2003 and 2010 with hunters from the northern part of Oyo State (widely identified as Òkè-Ògùn), satellite villages of Ibadan, and some parts of Osun State in Nigeria. These hunters came from both the guinea savannah and tropical rain forest. In Òkè-Ògùn, the hunters were based in Şakí, Tedé, Òjé-Owódé, Agúnrege, Òtu and Àgó-Àrẹ. In Ibadan, the hunters were based in villages such as Dálì, Olókùúta, Abà Ìsàlè, Ọ̀wọ́ Baálé, Tọ́lá, Ẹlẹ́nuṣónṣó, Kúṣeélá, Alápó, Akínẹ̀rín, Àjóyìnbọn, Ṣágbẹ and Aráròmí. In Osun State, the hunters came from Ìwó, Ìkirè, Ilé Ogbó, Ajagunlaàṣẹ, Ìgbínjẹ, Ifẹ̀ Ọ̀dàn and Látúndé. All the hunters, except two, were Yoruba of Nigeria. One of the non-Yoruba hunters was

Beninoise and the other Nupe. All the hunters and non-hunters were male, with ages ranging from 20 to 90.

The research employed a variety of field techniques, including observation, participant observation, focus group discussions, in-depth interviews, and key informant technique. Through key informants, I identified such occasions of hunters' activities as festivals and hunting expeditions; where possible, I participated. Each situation naturally suggested which method was used to elicit the data.

Since narratives typically ensue in the process of conversation, I frequently found myself in the position of encouraging the performance. I achieved this by exploiting the role of an interlocutor to ask questions, to exclaim, or to encourage the narrator whenever he pursued the narrative aspect. Most of the time, the discussions took place in informal and convivial settings in which the participants were relatively relaxed. In Òjé-Owódé, Ṣakí East Local Government, Oyo State, I participated for two weeks in the two-month-long communal hunting expedition and recorded certain aspects of the activity. I also participated in a communal Ògún worship and festival in Ìkirè, Osun State, and an individually organised Ògún festival in Òkè-Àdó, Oyo State.

I was statutorily excluded from some of the hunters' activities, including the hunters' weekly meeting. I observed these proceedings from a safe distance and debriefed hunter-informants after. Similarly, broadcast ethics kept me from participating actively in the narrative sessions observed in the radio studio. I simply listened to the narratives broadcast on the Broadcasting Corporation of Oyo State (BCOS) Radio1 hunters' narrative series, Ọdẹ Akọni, and watched those broadcast on Ọdẹ́tẹ̀dó on the BCOS television. Nevertheless, I was present in the radio studio for six of the broadcasts and was permitted to record three of the sessions on video and magnetic audio tape. Between 2003 and 2010, however, I carried out remote recording of 39 of the radio narratives using a transistor radio and cassette player/recorder set. By the end of 2004, Ọdẹ́tẹ̀dó, starting to falter for lack of sponsorship, was either broadcasting past editions or cancelling episodes outright. It was finally taken off the air in 2005. In 2009, I collected video tapes of seven past episodes of Ọdẹ́tẹ̀dó.

The attribution of specific geographical locations to those observed in the study is not without some qualification, as the hunter qua hunter thrives mainly on the trespass of all sorts of borders. I therefore sometimes met hunters in situations far from their native homes. Even when the hunters were in their native regions, the events they recounted were sometimes set either in forests or the bush far away from their homes or bases. For convenience, those hunters whose narratives and reflections are examined are identified either by the places where they live, the landscape they hunt or their native homes. Each of these designations is determined by the context of reference.

Since it is my purpose to use these performance narratives to interrogate certain generalisations typically used in describing cultural forms in Africa, specific consideration should be given not only to each cultural form but also to instances of its performance. One such form is the informal conversational narrative; the hunters' stories and their performances present us with forms of communication that diverge from several models taken for granted as fixed Yoruba cultural codes. Narratives as such abound in the recorded texts of the focus group discussions, as they do in those of the interviews. The Yoruba, like many other peoples, illustrate with narratives. This is especially important for the hunter because he describes an unfamiliar reality that demands some sort of domestic analogy for his audience to comprehend it. It is by situating his interpretation of reality in a specific narrative that the hunter makes his experience comprehensible.

Many hunters hold tenaciously to the belief that 'the hunter does not talk indiscreetly'. This is a maxim that forecloses the total narrativity of the hunter's experience; it prevents or at least tones down the ogreish and scary details of the Other. The hunter, is, in fact, a liminal facility whom society employs to do just this. Pa Ogunjimi of Aṣípa compound, Òjé-Owódé, when prompted to give an account of the experience of his hunting days, said: '*Ohun a bá rí n'íjù, kò séé sọ n'lé*' [Whatever is seen in the wild is better not recounted at home] and kept menacingly quiet for a moment before demurring:

> *Àmọ́ toò, ayé wáá d'ayé e ká f'ọ̀rọ̀ wàni l'ẹnu wò l'èyí t'áa sọ yìí. B' áa bá pé aá ròyìn ijù, b'áa bá l'ọ́mọ kékeé, kòníí lè lọ mọ́ . . . T'ọ́mọ bá kéré báyìí, t'áabá nròyìn ijù, t'ìṣẹ̀ ẹ baba a wá bá dé, t'áa bá gbe lé e l'ọ́wọ́, kò ní lè d'ẹnu odi.*

> [But now that everything in the world is being subjected to investigation, we may consider telling you some of the things . . . For when we reveal those things without caution, these children growing up (points at a group of children playing nearby) would be too scared to even go as far as the town's gate whenever they are called upon to take up their ancestral responsibility.][4]

Given this code of silence, it is not surprising that, in many cases, my requests for audience were simply turned down. Two elderly hunters, sought in two different locations, specifically grumbled about 'these Ibadan people' turning private hunting matters into radio business. Already indicted by my visible writing pad and recording gadgets, I could not convince these two men and others holding similar sentiments to agree to even an unrecorded interaction. Similarly, it was often difficult to obtain permission for recording and taking photographs. Many respondents who had earlier consented to being interviewed simply backed down when I showed up later with a camera and voice recorder. Some of these situations were, however, remedied by the assurance that the interaction could still happen 'off the record'.

Goldstein (1964) suggests three possible settings in which a performance could be observed: the 'natural', the 'artificial', and the 'induced natural'. The 'natural' setting suggested in Goldstein's category is desirable and suitable for the current study. At least in the very absolute sense, however, it proved impossible to produce. The hunter's narrative enterprise is conjoined with other aspects in the larger matrix of social communication. The narratives thereby often come up extempore, as an illustration of a lesson, explication of a point or just entertainment within conversation. It is exactly as inseparable from conversation as any other conversational narrative that presumes to report life. It is therefore overwhelmingly daunting, if not impossible, to identify in advance a situation of such a 'natural' performance and prepare to record it. Nevertheless, there were a couple of instances in which the performances were observed in such 'natural' settings. In general, however, both ethics and lack of preparation foreclosed the possibility of recording such a 'natural' performance. That most of the narratives considered for this work were prompted or, to use Goldstein's term, 'induced,' therefore threatens their absolute claim to 'naturalness'. However, my past unrecorded exposure to the natural settings through personal interaction is relied upon in the consideration of context.

The immediate aim of conducting video and audio recording of some of the field activities was to allow for subsequent study and analysis of the recorded data. A Sony TCM-150 voice recorder and an SVP DC-12V still photo and video camera were used. But these gadgets, as Jackson (1988) notes, heard and saw only what their handler made them hear and see. In fact, they heard and saw less than I did, who witnessed the narratives in the context of the hunters' larger culture. These gadgets have the additional adverse potential of making the informants and respondents 'sit up' and behave in a manner different from their usual ways (Okpewho 1983). I tried to mitigate these situations by engaging the respondents in friendly conversation until they thawed considerably and were more relaxed. And because the video camera magnifies this problem, I used it sparingly. Video recording was limited largely to such communal and corporate activities as expedition and ritual.

Age, the major determinant of seniority among the Yoruba, added yet another variable to the data collected. Barber (1991:183) observes the extent of the individual assertion of such seniority:

'You are a small boy to me', 'I had given birth even before you married', 'I was walking before you were born' are comments that are heard continually as hierarchy of seniority is produced in daily life.

This aspect of the culture comes with some subtle intimidation of the younger person from asserting himself before an audience of older people. At Òjé-Owódé, for example, one group of hunters was made up of six people, five of them between the ages of 65 and 85. The sixth person was a man of about 35 (see plates 1.4–1.8). Even as the five oldest participants were not of the same age, they performed their narratives without any fear of appearing boastful or arrogant before the elders. The situation was different for the youngest participant, Ògúnlékè, who was 'looking over his shoulders' throughout, and told no story except to briefly affirm what 'àwọn bàbá a wa' [our fathers] had said. In a discussion held with another group in Ibadan, the result was virtually the same, with the exception that an older hunter and his son occurred together as characters in a narrative performed by the former.

Plate 1.4: Ògúnjìmí

Plate 1.5: Jọ̀ọ́gún

Plate 1.6: Ọláògún

Plate 1.7: Ògúndélé

Plate 1.8: Ògúnlékè

Plate 1.9: Balọ́dẹ Lawal Ògúntúndé (left)

In Ṣakì, however, the method was deliberately redesigned to allow the younger hunters more licence. The hunters were approached individually, yet this approach also suffered a hitch. Òkèlọlá Julius, a man of about 50 and the first hunter approached, would not entertain any discussion until I had first spoken with Lamidi, his senior and the Balọ́dẹ of Ọ̀tún, Ṣakí. Lamidi, in turn, demanded that I brief the older Balọ́dẹ of Ọ̀tún, Ṣakí before he would make himself available (see plates 1.9–1.11). In response to their demands, the order of the individual discussion sessions was reversed, with the oldest respondent appearing first.

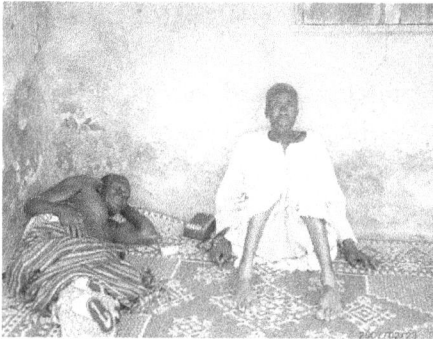

Plate 1.10: Balọ́dẹ Ọ̀tún Làsísì (seated, right)   Plate 1.11: Julius Òkèlọlá

Despite this small setback, the main objective of the discussions was realised. The hunters thus spoke with confidence, no matter their age. Consider, for example, an instance in which Balọ́dẹ Ọ̀tún Làsísì and Balọ́dẹ Lawal Ògúntúndé offered different opinions. Balọ́dẹ Ògúntúndé held that the '*ǹkẹnkíǹkẹn*' [odd things or spirits] existed in the long gone past. '*Àmá kò s'írú ẹ̀ mọ́ nîisìn 'í. Ǹkẹnkíǹkẹn ò sí mọ́. Gbogbo ẹ̀ ni ọkọ̀ọ̀ ti lé lọ*' [But there are no more such things today. Odd things are no more. Automobile has driven them all away]. Làsísì, oblivious of the claim of the older Balọ́dẹ, to whom he would always defer, responded to my query about whether spirits exist as follows:

> *Às'ọ́mọ kékeré ni ọ́, ọ̀ọ̀ mọ nkẹnkẹn . . . T'ẹ́ẹ̀ npé n'gbà ọkọ̀ọ̀ pọ̀, òórùn ọkọ̀ [lé wọn lọ]; irọ́ ni o. Wọ́n n bẹ o. Wọ́n n bẹ o. Wọ́n bẹ o.*

> [You are such a naïve youth . . . Some do say the smell of automobile [has driven them away]; that is not true. They still exist. They exist. They do exist.]

Six of the narratives collected for the study have been transcribed (see appendices A–F). The transcription emasculates the oral performance. No amount of annotation can redeem the performativity of an oral narrative reduced to writing. But transcription nevertheless mitigates the immediate problem of literary analysis of performance. The transcription takes into consideration the individual and dialectal peculiarities of all the narrators and respondents, and tries to set them down accordingly. No attempt is made to re-convey the narrators' and other respondents' words in 'standard' Yoruba. Rather, the transcription attempts to represent the words as they were articulated.

Notes

1. Recorded interview, 17/04/2007.

2. Recorded interview, 16/12/2006.

3. Personal interaction, 30/11/2002.

4. Personal interaction, 16/12/2006.

2

Art, the Hunter's World and Death of Fixity

Introduction

Like all forms of informal art, Yoruba hunters' narratives resist easy categorisation. Categorising the narratives as either fact or fiction proves difficult and in fact inappropriate, owing more to Western notions of cultural dualism than African worldviews. After introducing various components of the hunter's narrative as an art form, this chapter explores how praxis upsets taxonomy. It concludes with a reflection on how the dualist epistemological obsession with myth and reality has distorted the understanding of African art forms.

The performance art of hunters' narratives

Hunters' narratives are the stories of the hunters' exploits in the forest. They are essentially no different from narratives that emanate from regular conversations, but their thematic engagement of the weird, the magical and the uncanny ensures the listener's curiosity and attention in a manner that stories by, say, barbers, blacksmiths and weavers do not. Always taking people away from the immediate and the known, the stories told by and of hunters are also a literary infrastructure in many folktales. However, it is as a report of real-life encounters that the hunters' narratives acquire prime audience. Though the hunter's narrative has no specific nomenclature, it is a form with which every Yoruba person is familiar, either told as a story in itself or infused as a sub-narrative in another genre. Today, the broadcast media have different narrative and chit-chat programmes that feature the hunters' stories. Conversation among such users of the Yoruba language as the hunters is in itself art, particularly with the potential that the interlocutors could break into autopanegyric *oríkì* or *ìjálá*. This is another point where for both the narrator of folktales and the story-teller of twentieth century stories, such as Fagunwa (1949,

1950a, 1950b, 1954, 1961), or radio host Kọ́lá Akíntáyọ̀, the hunter persona constitutes a ready resource.

In part because the hunters' narratives traditionally take the form of informal conversation, they do not immediately come across as a conscious art. Tedlock (1977:515) notes that among the Quiche Maya of New Mexico, 'stories occur to people only when conversation or chance events bring them to mind: they never set aside an occasion for them. In the midst of a conversation about crocodiles and iguana, someone says, "Well, there's a story about that" and proceeds to tell it on the spot'. But even in this context, the narrator deploys various verbal devices to ensure 'captivation of audience, retention of audience and the transfer of cognitive experience to the audience' (Sekoni 1990:140), so much so that the ensuing product often qualifies as a work of art. The hunter's narrative in this manner frequently uses existing figural devices, such as *ìbà*, proverb, *oríkì* and *ọfò*.

Ìbà (Acknowledgement and appeal)

Ìbà is the Yoruba expression of acknowledgement and/or admission of inferiority before powerful human and supernatural forces. As part of songs and poetry, the performer's intention is to appease the identified class of superordinates in order to appropriate their power or forestall antagonism (Isola 1976). *Ìbà* occurs in the performance of many of the hunters' narratives. In the radio programme *Ọdẹ Akọni* especially, which tends towards a formal structure because of its broadcast format, *ìbà* is a regular introduction. Chanted as *ìjálá* or voiced in speech mode, the host, before the narrative session commences, often addresses *ìbà* to the following forces: God, man, woman, *àjé*, nature, deities and legendary representations of certain ideas of value to hunting and elocution. At the foreground of the *ìjálá* refrain, sung in the form of *fújí* (a modern Yoruba musical form that emerged from the Islamic rites of Ramadan), Akíntáyọ̀, the presenter of *Ọdẹ Akọni,*. commences the day's programme with a flattering submission to Olódùmarè:

> Ọló'un ọba à mi, mọ màmà tún dé o. Èmi tí n ọ̀ mọ̀ ọ́ wí rè é, t'Ọló'un Ọba à mi maá n báá wí i ní gbogbo Sunday-Sunday . . . Toò, èmi tí n ọ̀ jẹ́ nkankan rèé o, Ọló'un Ọba à mi ìbà.

> [O God my King, here I am again, bereft of eloquence but always given voice by God himself every Sunday . . . Here I am nothing before him . . . God I pay homage.]

Thereafter, Akíntáyọ̀ always acknowledges the genus man and the *àjé*:

> Mo tún júbà ọkùn'in, mo júbà obìnrin. Mọ wá júbà ẹyin àjẹẹ Tẹ́ẹ̀rì t'ẹ nj'áyé o: ẹ̀yin abapá wẹẹ, abẹsẹ̀ wẹẹ, abìrìn àsà l'ẹ́sẹ̀ mejèèjì, ẹ káalẹ́ sẹ́ẹ̀.

[Now I pay homage to man and to woman. I then pay homage to the àjẹ́ of Tẹ́ẹ̀rì, the mysterious ones: you the sleight-handed and the flight-footed ones of the elegant walk, good evening].[1]

The hunter naturally covets any power, skill and luck that would predispose him to killing animals every day. *Ìkookò*, the wolf, is one of the hunter's embodiments of such endowment. The hunters suppose that in the mythical past, *Ìkookò* had consulted Kíndìnrín and Jàndímọ́lẹ̀, both *babaláwo*, for a ritual that has since invested him with the power to kill animals for food on daily basis. So Akíntáyọ̀ the hunter often appeals to the same team of diviners:

> *Ìbà Kíìndìnrín awo Ìdọ̀ha, Jàndímọ́lẹ̀ awo Ìlàrẹ́: àwọn ni wọ́n tẹ̀ 'Kookò n'fá tí ò fi gbọdọ̀ j'ẹran kàsì.*

[Homage to Kíndìnrín the diviner of Ìdọ̀ha and Jàndímọ́lẹ̀ the diviner of Ìlàrẹ́:[2] these were the ones who performed the ritual for Wolf so that he {killed every day and therefore} does not have to eat stale meat.][3]

Because the Yoruba hunter operates within a gerontocentric society, he measures his own formidability by the power of the master-hunter to whom he pays homage. An *Ìbà* to such a master-hunter is composed to flaunt the hunter's rich pedigree. At two points in his narrative, Kọbọmọjẹ Alade pauses to acknowledge one Chief Pọ́ríkú to whom he credits his survival of many daring expeditions.[4] In the narrative of Moses Ògúnwálẹ̀, the narrator describes the hunter's amazement at seeing the small deer he felled earlier grow larger. The premonition of the coming danger compels him to invoke his father and master, and other allied powers. At that point in the performance, the performative energy invested in the *ìbà* relocates it from the fictive realm of the past to the here-and-now. Ògúnwálẹ̀, in that performance, exploits the *ìbà* scene evoked in the narrative not just to relive the event but to pay homage. The host of the programme tries to stop him to keep the focus on the story, but Ògúnwálẹ̀ ignores him and continues:

> *Kò níí sòro ó se. Mọ bá f'ìbà sí i. Mo júbà baba à mi. Adélẹ́kàn Àjàó. Ọrún u're rẹ o. Ìbà: okó t'ó dorí kodò tí 'ò ro; ìbà: iyámọ̀pó t'ó d'orí kodò tí 'ọ̀ s'ẹ̀jẹ̀. Ìbà ni ń ọ maa f'òní jú. Má jẹ́ẹ́ ó sú mi í se o. Má jẹ n sìse n bẹ̀ o. Má j'átùpà Ògún ó t'ìdí jò mọ́ n lọ́'ọ́ o.*

[There would be no problem. I paid homage. I paid homage to my father Adelekan Ajao. May your heavenly rest be peaceful. Homage to the penis that droops and yet does not drip and the vagina that opens downward and yet does not bleed. Homage shall I pay you all for the whole day. Do not let me tire. Do not let me fail. Save me from the accidental burst of the Ògún lamp {gun}.]

Proverb

Proverb is one of the most exploited devices of elocution among the Yoruba and also in most African cultures. It is employed not only in the formal arts of poetry, singing and drumming, but also in conversation (Olatunji 1984). It is inevitably a major device in the performance of the hunters' narratives, the most recurrent being '*Tí ọdẹ bá ro iṣẹ, ti ọdẹ bá ro ìyà, t'ó bá p'ẹran, kò níí f'ẹnìkankan*' [If the hunter takes stock of all his adversities, he would share his kill with no one]. As considered here, the Yoruba *òwe*, or proverb, is not a cold tablet of inherited aphorisms, but rather a short, witty figural expression employed, modified, and/or composed to convey the message of the performer. There is a sense in which the Yoruba may see an entire length of narrative as an *òwe*, synonymous in that sense with parable.

Músílíù Àlàgbé Fìríàáríkú (see Appendix A) begins his narrative with the hint that the protagonist's supernatural power saves him from peril, using a statement half literal, half figural: '*Bí ọ bá jẹ pé mo múra lọ'ọ látinúu'lé pé n'torí aìímọ, áàh!* eégún ọdẹ ò bá fẹẹ̀ gbé ọjẹ n'jọ náà o' [Had I not equipped myself properly from home, *the hunter's masquerade would have perished in the grove that day*]. The metaphor in which the proverb is couched – the idea of masquerade perishing in the grove – reflects the dialectic coexistence of man the hunter and the forest. The hunter is destined to explore the forest as the *egúngún* belongs in *ọjẹ*, the primal grove. But the way is fraught with peril and he has to depend on his individual sagacity to negotiate his passage.

There is an instance of a proverb commonly employed in the narratives of Ajísefínní Alájáníbon of Ìdó, Ìbàdàn, and Àmẹẹdì Kókó-by-this of Òkè Ọbà, Ìwo:

1. **Ajísefínní:** *Ẹn' bá l'ówùú ọ t'ẹrù, ìwọn tí èe tanná ló mú. Òògùn n bẹ. Gbogbo ẹnu n mo e sọ ọ; òògùn nbẹ.*

   [Whoever considers the cotton wool light carries just the little he needs as wick. There are magical powers. I confidently say so; there are magical powers.]

2. **Kókó-by-this:** *Mélòò l'aá sọ n'núu'gbó? Iṣẹ ọdẹ 'ò easy . . . Torí ẹni t'ọ bá ní òwú ọ t'ẹrù, hun tí e e tanná ló mú.*

   [How much can one recount in the forest experience? Hunting is not easy . . . For whoever considers the cotton wool light carries the little needed as wick.]

The proverb draws its primary logic from the observation that cotton is as heavy as brick, ton for ton. The proverb's reference to the supposed lightness of cotton gestures to its availability in small pocket quantities; those who ply cotton in large quantities know the truth. Both the narratives of Ajísefínní and Kókó-by-this favour the character of the hunter; they empower him so that he always emerges triumphant. When prompted, Ajísefínní confirms that hunters have magical powers they use to fight off antagonists. But, most importantly, he considers such a question unnecessary; to him, the answer is patent enough, except to those who, like me, do not know the hunter well enough, that is, those who come by cotton wool in pocket quantities. As a narrator, Kókó-by-this not only exudes the hunter's confidence and pride, but also virtually demands that the audience know and acknowledge him. The proverb as employed in his preliminary statement instructs that the forest transcends absolute narrativity. It is by implying that the forest landscape is not totally narratively navigable that he as a hunter and a habitué of that landscape stands out in relief. He therefore follows the proverb with 'Àwọbọ yàtọ̀ sí àjẹbí. Wọ́n jẹ ẹ́ bí mi ni' [Learning a trade is different from being born into it. I was born into it].

The hunter not only appropriates and modifies proverbs; he also generates his own epigrams. Epigrams, too, should be considered as falling within the category of the Yoruba òwe. In his appearance on Ọdẹ Akọni, Akínkúnmi Akéwejè uses both known proverbs and extempore original epigrams. He points out at the end of the conflict in his first narrative that 'b'írin bá kan'rin ni àwọn t'án bí wa ma nwí, ìkan ó tẹ̀ fún 'kan' ['when two irons are locked in a fight', so say our fathers, 'the weaker gives way'] to simply connote that the hunter vanquishes the antagonist because the former is stronger. Akéwejè also apparently uses original epigrams, as none of the persons interacted with in the course of this study were familiar with his phrases. Most tellingly, the context of their performance shows their originality: they are generated, in part, from the very questions asked by the interlocutor:

Akíntáyò:	Ṣé'gi lè sọ̀rọ̀ ni t'ẹẹfi ní 'ò fún u yín lési?
Akéwejè:	Hẹn, b'áa bá f'igi lu'gi, à maa gbó'hùn u'gi.
Akíntáyò:	Ṣ'ódò lè sọ̀rọ̀?
Akéwejè:	B'éèyàn bá wẹ d'énú odò, odò ọ́ sọ̀rọ̀.
[Akíntáyò:	Does a tree speak? Why did you accuse the tree of not responding?
Akéwejè:	When you speak the language of the tree, you hear the tree speak.
Akíntáyò:	Does a river speak?
Akéwejè:	If you swim upriver enough, you hear the river speak.][5]

Translated literally, the first epigram reads, 'when you hit one tree with another, you hear the voice of the tree'. It denotes that attuning mundane human facilities to the language of the flora and fauna first requires the acquisition of spiritual or magical powers which the *igi* [tree] (i.e. herbs) represents in Yoruba. The idea of 'swimming upriver enough' is another reference to the hunter's ability to speak with nature. After all, the hunter and said river, according to the story, are such close friends that one does not betray the other.

Beyond appropriating, modifying, and creating witty sayings, the hunter sometimes undermines existing proverbs. By creating a trope of rebellious divergence, the hunter's stature as a maker of new myth rises. Consider, for instance, another saying of Kókó-by-this that verges on profanity in its engagement of an existing proverb. The Yoruba believe that when a fleeing deer barks like a dog, it magically eludes the hunter for that day, hence the saying '*Ijó àgbònrín bá gbó l'ojó ikú u rè é yè*' [When the deer barks, it postpones its death]. In the narrative of Kókó-by-this, the hunter defies the barking deer:

> *Wón ní'jó tí àgbònrín bá gbó, n'jó náà l'ojó ikú èé yè. N'jó tí àgbònrín bá gbó l'ódò mi, n'jó náá l'ojóo 'kúu è pé.*
>
> [It is said that when the deer barks, it postpones the day of its death. When a deer sees me and barks, it dies that very day.][6]

It is in the juxtaposition of the existing proverb and its subversive review that the hunter thus advances a personal myth.

Raji-Oyelade (1999:75) dubs this Yoruba subversive temper 'post-proverbial', by which he refers to 'the effect of the interplay of orality and literacy-modernity, the critical correspondence between an older puritanistic generation and younger disruptive and somewhat banalistic generation'. While it is certainly the case that the subversion of proverbs is particularly popular among Yoruba youth, it is important to point out that Yoruba culture, Raji-Oyelade's focus, tolerates modification and subversion not only of seemingly set linguistic idioms, but also of revered icons and institutions. There are existing proverbs with in-built caveats that seem to initiate their own review. One example is: '*Ogun àwíté̩lè̩ kìí p'aro {tó bá gbón}*' [Alerted early, a {wise} cripple flees and survives the war].

Oríkì

Yoruba *oríkì* is the poetic description, essentially panegyric, of a man, an animal, a place or an object. Barber (1991), using the Yoruba town of Òkukù as a case study, notes that *oríkì* have evolved around both individuals and lineages. The individual genius, expectedly, plays a role in the composition of personal *oríkì* among the

Yoruba hunters. An average Yoruba hunter has a set of personal praise names and epithets that he readily loads into the extempore praise of either himself or any other person or thing at any opportune moment. As a matter of course, the hunter's attempt to relate his story includes the regular declamation of personal *oríkì*. Regularly on *Ọdẹ Akọni*, Akíntáyọ̀, apart from invoking his lineage *oríkì*, 'Ìkìrun Àgùnbé Onílẹ̀ Obì', salutes himself with about half a dozen other praise names, including: '*Irúnmọlẹ̀ tíí gbé'gboro; kóóko l'ódò ab'àwọ̀ lọ̀ọ̀lọ̀*' [The spirit that lives in town; the lush grass of the river side]; '*Ọ̀jọ̀gbọ́n oníìjálá tíí yin aré Ògún bí ìbọn*' [The learned *ìjálá* poet that fires the Ògún performance like gunshot]; and '*Sèdíwonkokokóògùnsí, ọkọ Sàádátù*' [He-whose-haggard-waist-is-used-to-carry-charms, the husband of Sàádátù].

Ògúnkúnlé Òjó of Agúnrege hardly lets a mention of his wife or any of his children pass without an *oríkì* to it. When asked about what became of the buffalo that he fought in his narrative, he answers partly in poetry:

> *Mo fi nkan a'nú ẹ̀ bó'ta. Ìyàwó ò mi, Áfúsátù onísàasùn ẹja, abitan bí afárá oyin, tó m'ọbẹ̀ ẹ́ sè, tó m'ọwọ́ ọ síbí í gbámú, òhun náà tún jẹ n'nú ẹ̀.*

[I ate it with relish. My wife, Afusatu of the pot of fish stew, she of the sexy thighs who is a perfect cook, also ate some of it.][7]

When asked to give his name, Agbọọlá Alájáníbọn Détunhà says:

> *Emì ni Ògúndélé Oníjìngín-ìbọn Alájáníbọn, Ikútíídẹ́tunhà baba Dúpẹ́. Ọ pà'yá ọ̀dúndún tán ọmọ rẹ̀ n s'ọjọ̀jọ̀. Mo tún gbìyànjú mo tún m'ọmọọ rẹ̀ w'ábà.*

[I am Ògúndélé, He-of-the-decorated-gun, He-who-has-both-dogs-and-guns, Death-that-breaks-the-duiker's-ribs, the father of Dúpẹ́. I kill the mother monkey and its baby pines. So I take the baby to the village alive.][8]

The presenter of *Ọdẹ Akọni*, even as he assumes the role of an audience, frequently directs his queries and observations in attempts to rein in the guest performer to a linear narrative course. Yẹkínì Oláwuyì Omítóògùn Améringùn, the fiery protagonist of his own narrative, has little patience for such oversight. As the host persistently pressures him to return to the point of the story where the protagonist takes possession of the gourdlets and the pebbles found in the deer, Ameringun asserts himself with intimidating *oríkì* chanted in *ìjálá*:

> *Farabalẹ̀! Farabalẹ̀! Farabalẹ̀! Ẹ̀ẹse wẹ̀?*
> *Èmi lo rí lò n pè l'ẹ́nìkan*
> *[ìjálá] Èmi dá'kún jẹ má f'àágbà ọdẹ jẹ*
> *Apabíaláwọ̀n, baba Ògúnmọ́dẹdé*

[Take it easy! Easy! Easy! What is wrong with you?
{*Ìjálá*} You see me yet you take me for just one man
I who killed and ate the ground squirrel without giving
the elder-hunter a share
I who kill animals in multitude as if by dragnet, the father of Ògúnmọ́dẹdé][9]

The *oríkì* becomes a momentary device for intimidation, appealing to his authority as one who defied the elder hunter without suffering any repercussions.

Hunters' narratives also invoke *oríkì* of animals. Ògúnkúnlé Òjó, in the narrative of his confrontation with a buffalo, praises the animal antagonist: '*Ògbó ọmọ Akùmárọ̀; afínjú on'sàngó tíí so kele ti'ẹ̀ m'ẹ̀sẹ̀ òsì* [Ògbó the child of Akùmárò; the fashionable votary of Sango that puts its *kele*[10] beads on the left ankle].[11]

Ọfọ̀ incantation

Ọfọ̀ is the poetry that accompanies magical invocation or medication (Olatunji 1984). Often composed to argue the 'logic' in the invocation or medication, *ọfọ̀* chant is a performance form that the hunter uses to prevent or hold off adversity. Beyond merely reliving the process of invocation as an experience, the hunter-narrator's re-enactment of the *ọfọ̀* is intended to show off his education in such matters. In the narrative of Bílíámínù Babátúndé Ajíjàagùn performed by Kọ́lá Akíntáyọ̀, the protagonist enchants a quarrelsome spirit and makes him drink palwine to a state of stupor with the following *ọfọ̀*:

Kíndìnrín awo Ìdọ̀ha
Jàndímọ́lẹ̀ awo Ìlàrẹ́
Àwọn ni'án tẹ̀'Kookò n'fá, tí ọ gbọdọ̀ j'ẹran kàsì
Gbogbo ọ̀rọ̀ tí òkété bá b'álẹ̀ sọ n'ilẹ̀ ẹ́ gbọ́ . . .
O ó mu ú ni. O ọ̀ gbọdọ̀ bá n jà
Torípé wọn èé ka léégúnlóko kún'gi ilé
Wọn èé k'ẹ̀ẹ̀rù kún nkan ọbẹ
Wọn èé k'alángbá k'ẹran orí àtẹ

[Kindinrin the diviner of Ìdọ̀ha
Jandimole the diviner of Ìlàré
These were the ones who performed the ritual for Wolf
so that he does not eat stale meat
Whatever the giant rat tells the land, the land heeds . . .
Drink you must. Do not quarrel with me
For no one uses léégúnlóko wood to build house
Ẹ̀ẹ̀rù is no ingredient for cooking soup
No one puts up the meat of agama lizard for sale]

The performance of the *ọfọ̀* portrays Akíntáyọ̀, the present narrator, as learned in magic and charms, even more than it presents Ajíjàagùn himself as the hero. The point is not lost on the audience that Akíntáyọ̀ is the author of the present text. If Ajíjàagùn ever used the *ọfọ̀* at all, the present narrator would also have the listener believe he also knows and uses it. Moreover, the first three lines of the chant usually recur in the presenter's *ìbà* opening of *Ọdẹ Akọni*. The *ọfọ̀* is therefore one action in the performance through which the third-person performer shares glory with the hero.

Apart from the *ọfọ̀* employed in the conflict in his story, Yẹ̀kínì Omítóògùn Améringùn's performance on *Ọdẹ Akọni* presents a peculiar example of the *ọfọ̀* as a mnemonic of narration. When asked not to forget the point where he earlier stopped in the narration before the commercial break, he breaks into *ọfọ̀* intoned in ìjálá:

> *Èyíi mọ bá gbàgbé*
> *Eéran wọn ọ́ maa rán mi l'étí gaanrangan*
> *B'ákùkọ bá gbọnpá, iyè e rẹ̀ yíó sì sọ*

> [Whatever I forget
> Let *eéran*, the agent of recollection, bring it back
> Every time the rooster flaps its wings, its senses wake][12]

Améringùn, the narrator, thereby presumes to have enlisted some muse of recollection that will ensure the narrative exposition of every necessary detail.

In the televised narrative of Olú Oyèwùmí, the *ọfọ̀*, itself sourced from the *odù* of *Ifá*, establishes a sublime parallel narrative. In the larger narrative, the protagonist is frustrated in his bid to kill animals in an unnamed forest: 'Ìrókò *kan ń bẹ ń'núu'gbó hun, tí n bá ti dé'bẹ̀ báyìí, wàhálà ọ́ bẹ̀rẹ̀. Kò ní jẹ́ kí n rí àwọn ẹran yẹn pa*' [There was an *ìrókò*[13] in that forest that always gave me trouble. It would not let me kill the animals].[14] It is in the ritual warding off of the *ìrókò* checkmate that the metanarrative emerges. In that narrative *ọfọ̀*, the hunter returns as a protagonist who is waylaid and quizzed by a Yoruba archdeity, Ọbàtálá:

> *B'érin bá jẹ'ko tán, á f'eyín lu'yín ke, ke, ke*
> *B'ẹ́fọ̀n ba jẹ'ko tán, a f'ìwo lù'wo gbàn, gbàn, gbàn*
> *Mọ bọ́'áàrin ọ̀nà, mo b'Óòsà Ńlá kan t'ó f'ìkóódẹ há rí tantan*
> *Ó n''Ìwọ ọmọ ta nùun'*
> *Mo l''Émi ọmọ Òrígìrìsayọ̀'*
> *Ó l''Òrígìrìsayọ̀ t'ìlú u yín ńkọ́?'*
> *Mo l''Éwé Olúkánikò ọ́ bá mi ká a kò'*
> *Ó l''Ọ̀nà wo ní ọ́ gbà ká a kò?'*
> *Mo ní 'Bíbú l'ọ̀ràn á bú ń'nú àgbá.'*
> *Ijọ́ ògúlúǹtu bá bọ́ lulẹ̀ l'ọ̀ran a'nú ẹ ẹ́ túká.*

Ọ̀nàá gbàjá o, ọ̀nàá r'òkun
Ọ̀nàá gbàjá o, ọ̀nàá r'ọ̀sà
Ìrìn ire n mo rìn, n 'ò rin ti kùnmọ̀
T'óo bá l'ẹran l'ọbẹ̀ k'óo fún mi jẹ.'
Ìrìn ire n mo rìn, n 'ò rin ti kùnmọ̀.

[When elephants are done with grazing, they clink their tusks,
one against the other
When the buffaloes are done with grazing, they knock their horns,
one against the other
In the middle of my way, I met an Ọbàtálá[15] with the tail-feather
of a parrot stuck fast in his head
He asked me, 'Whose son are you?'
I answered, 'I the son of Òrígìrìsayọ̀.' [He-who-thrives-in-trouble.]
He asked, 'What of the other Òrígìrìsayọ̀ of your town?'
I said, 'The binder's leaf will bind him for me.'
He asked me 'Through what means will it bind him?'
I said, 'When the charge gets into a barrel, it explodes.'
For the day the brickbat falls from a height, the trouble within it
shatters with it
The road puts on its girdle and journeys to the sea
The road puts on its girdle and journeys to the lagoon
I, wayfarer, come in peace, I deserve no punishment
He who has meat in his soup, give me some
I, wayfarer, come in peace, I deserve no punishment.]

The interview obviously ends in the protagonist's favour, foreshadowing his victory. But the foreshadowing so significantly and comprehensively implies what will come that Oyewumi, the performing hunter, deploys just a single sentence as a literal explication of the conflict that the *ọfọ̀* poetry idiomatises: '*Mọ wọ́ ǹkan à mi gẹẹrẹgẹ*' [I reached out and seized my kill]. The immediate television audience are so involved as co-performers of the incantation that they need no expatiation. The narrator simply moves on to a description of the conflict that follows the next day.

Ìjálá, Ìrèmọ̀jé and the hunter's allergy to fixity

The allure of structuralism that pervaded most disciplines in cultural studies for much of the late twentieth century has had dramatic effects on how those cultures were assessed. Even in cases where critics were not necessarily allied with the structuralist tradition, the influence of two important aspects of structuralist thought, namely, fascination with binaries and opposites, and positivism, were overwhelming. For studies of African culture, this structuralist orientation has yielded an unhealthy fascination with categorising narratives as either myth or reality – a theme to which I shall return later. But the structuralist attitude has had more pervasive, and less obvious, influence in its insistence between text and context, between norms and deviation from norms.

De Saussure set the template for these binary assumptions with his work in linguistics. He distinguished between *la langue*, the system which underlies the practice of language, and *la parole*, individual instances of speech actions (De Saussure 1988:77). Despite the attention paid to the definition of *la parole*, subsequent studies of African cultural forms neglected *la parole* in favour of *la langue*. Even while recognising this situation, Anozie (1981) cautions that critical enterprise should not lose sight of the *norms* whose existence performance, even as an exercise in negation, presupposes. He nevertheless acknowledges the need to go beyond the dualist conceptualisations of orthodox structuralism. For Anozie (1981:235), remedy comes in the form, on the one hand, of studying speech acts as performance, and, on the other, through the 'tendency of poststructuralism towards theoretical flexibility'. Even so, Anozie's approach to African art forms – for instance, his insistence that masks may be understood as artefacts isolated from the masquerade and the festival arena – reveals a deep-seated attachment to a text/ context dichotomy. He virtually presumes that *that* context in literary analysis is secondary in importance to the text. With particular reference to the work of Anozie, Appiah has pointed out the failure of Saussurean linguistics in neglecting the study of *la parole*. It is characteristic of the structuralist tradition, Appiah (1981) writes, to see language as one linear discourse, not paying attention to the disjunction that a close study of praxis exposes.

The earliest attempts at describing the Yoruba hunter as an agent of cultural performance somewhat minimise the hunter's potential for performative modification and subversion of cultural hegemony. The accounts of both Babalola (1966) and Àjùwòn (1980, 1982) are representative. They both are commentaries on the more normative verbal arts of the hunters: *ìjálá* and *ìrèmòjé*. In *The content and form of Yoruba Ìjálá*, Babalola (1966:3) defines the hunters' performance of poetry as 'aré Ògún (the entertainment of the god Ògún)':

> the performers are referred to as *àwọn aláré Ògún* (those who perform Ògún's entertainment) . . . Hunters predominate among the worshippers of the god Ògún, and with this is connected the belief that Ògún in his early life was a hunter and that as a god he is the controller of all iron implements, including guns, cutlasses, and swords.

Babalola's work gives insight on the origin narratives, contexts of performance and the thematic preoccupation of the *ìjálá*.

Similarly, in a series of publications, Àjùwòn (1980; 1981; 1982) dwells on *ìrèmòjé*, the Yoruba hunter's poetry performance preliminary to *ìsípà*, the hunter's funeral rites. Writing on the importance of the entire funeral rite, of which *ìrèmòjé* is an aspect, Àjùwòn (1982:20) notes that the rites represent 'to the Yoruba hunters a final separation of the deceased hunter from the earthly hunters' guild. It is the hunters' belief that once the deceased hunter finally loses his membership in the hunters' earthly guild, he shall no longer hunt with the living hunters.'

Why do living hunters have to commit time and resources to terminating interaction with the dead, since all hunters straddle the spiritual and the physical realms in any case? Considering that the hunter's encounter with spirits, sometimes of the dead, is often anything but friendly, he finds it more agreeable to redefine relations with one's own dead so that they find their rightful place as ancestors to whom the living hunters must relate as superiors instead of joining the sundry footloose spirits that trouble earthly hunters (Àjùwòn 1982).

Both Babalola and Àjùwòn are, in effect, proposing that the hunters' performance of poetry must be understood as particular forms: as entertainment for Ògún, in the case of Babalola, and as funerary poetry, in the case of Àjùwòn. These theses are adequate to the extent that they do not presuppose absolutes. Today, however, when a person reads some of Babalola's observations on the texts and contexts of *ìjálá* performance, it is easy to come up with available examples that challenge his taxonomy. According to Babalola (1966:25): 'It is sad to record that nowadays, in their bid to outshine one another at social gatherings, *some* ìjálá *artists shamelessly and deliberately corrupt the traditional text of [the]* oríkì orílè *chants*' [my italics].

Later in the same chapter, Babalola (1966:38–39) explains that he

> will exclude the examples of those vulgar jokes which many an *ìjálá* artist, in order to excite laughter, nonchalantly resorts to, especially when he is tipsy and unashamed to chant lewd remarks and indecent narratives' because such broad humour is not usually found in the chants of elderly *ìjálá*-chanters, who employ euphemism in their references to sexual organs and sexual life.

Two separate issues arise from this statement. First, Babalola's decision to exclude 'lewd' behaviour illustrates the official tyranny of labelling a cultural behaviour as 'rogue' because it does not follow the normative trajectory. Second, there is no proof that what the writer considers 'lewd' or 'vulgar' is not, after all, a canonical example. Contrary to Babalola's first objection, the Yoruba *oríkì* and *oríkì orílè* are not set in stone. Their performativity as *ìjálá* or any other form undermines their fixity. Besides, *oríkì* is partly a commentary on man and life and, to this extent, is documentary. The continuity and dissonance from which poetry draws its breath therefore presupposes that it constantly renews itself. Furthermore, though the *oríkì orílè* is a communal cultural resource, the individual has access to it as raw material in the composition of his or her own *oríkì*. Barber (1991:250) puts it aptly:

> *oríkì orílè* belong collectively to a group, but they are usually addressed to individuals. The group emblem is thus bound up intimately with individual self-consciousness and self-display, and performance is to enhance the individual against the background of – even at the expense of – other, rival individuals. Individual identity is constituted out of communal identity: and at the same time it is through the salutation of the individual that group identity is reaffirmed. Because there is gradual absorption of *oríkì* into *oríkì orílè*, individual idiosyncrasy, even the most trivial, can become part of the symbolic self-representation of the group.

For the Yoruba hunter, this site where the composition of the individual myth engages the so-called fixity of *oríkì orílè* in what could be termed a dialectic of tradition and change, proves convenient. Mythmaking is stretched, sometimes almost to a point of profanity. Such liberties are, after all, part of the hunter's search for novelty as a means to highlight the self, the hero.

Two queries highlight the problematic assumptions embedded in Babalola's decision to exclude 'lewd' texts:

1. Does ìjálá draw from the *oríkì orílè*? The answer to this is evidently 'yes', as evidenced by Babalola's own data and narrative.

2. Are there *oríkì orílè* with 'lewd remarks and indecent narratives' in them? The answer is also the affirmative. The following *oríkì orílè* text is a good example:

> *Ọmọ Ìyániwúrà ni Gògò*
> *Ẹni t'óbìnrin wò sùnsùn t'ó bú s'ẹ́kún*
> *T'ó ní bí eléyìí 'ò bá jé ọkọ ẹni, a sì j'álè ẹni*
> *Ọmọ òtọrọ-ọbẹ̀-tọrọ-abẹ*
> *Àgbà tí ò l'ọ́bẹ̀ kó m'ábẹ́ wá*
> *Torí pé abẹ́ dùn ó j'ọbẹ̀ lọ*
> *Ọmọ òtọrọ-ọbẹ̀-tọrọ-abẹ*
> *Àgbà tí 'ò l'ọ́bẹ̀, ẹ sọ fún u kó m'ábẹ́ ẹ̀ wá*
> *Nítorí abẹ́ yó ní o j'oǹjẹ lọ.*

> [Son of Ìyániwúrà in Gògò
> A man that a woman regards lustfully and breaks into tears of frustration
> Wishing she could be his lover if not his wife
> He who begs for soup and begs for sex as well
> A woman who has no soup could give me her genitals
> For sex is more pleasant than soup

He who begs for soup and begs for sex as well
Tell the woman who has no soup to bring forth her genitals
For the genitals are more satisfying than food.][16]

Today, the two most popular living *ìjálá* artists are Ògúndáre Fóyánmu and Àlàbí Ògúndépò. Elsewhere, I argue that the performance of Àlàbí Ògúndépò is by far the more daring of the two in its upsetting of known generic terms (Adeduntan 2003). According to Babalola's (1966: 38–39) definitions, Fóyánmu's art would, at least in relation to Ògúndépò, represent 'the chant of elderly *ìjálá*-chanters, who employ euphemism in their references to sexual organs and sexual life' and in whose poetry 'broad humour is not usually found'. But here, account must be taken of the context of the performance, particularly the official partitioning of the idioms of public and the private spaces. A language that is, for example, tabooed in the media is held as aberrant, and even deficient in what that language seeks to express. The 'formal' idiom of the media is therefore confused with the native idiom of the narratives broadcast on them. On radio and television, for example, the censor suppresses 'the offensive' – though the so-called 'offensive' paradoxically permeates the extra-media everyday public life. The *oríkì orílè* cited above and the following text from Foyanmu's albums, *Igbaladun Tabętabę* (n.d.), could be read in this light:

Dàpò Ìsòlá o bó ló'ò ayé
Irun ìsàlè bó lò'ò onídìrí o
O bó ló'ò ayé

[Dàpò Ìsòlá, you are now free from the world
Just as the pubic hair has eluded the hairdresser
You are free from the world]

This is the musical refrain in the piece the poet composed to mourn his late drummer. Even in this example, the metaphor has been toned down under the surveillance of the Censors Board. The *ìjálá* refrain is taken from the repertoire of existing hunters' songs. The '*irun ìsàlè*' [literally 'the hair below'] of Fóyánmu's text is often otherwise rendered '*irun òbò*' [literally 'hair of the vagina'].

In one episode of *Odętèdò*, a hunter listener broke into song during a phone-in, using the well-known '*irun òbò*' version.[17] Ordinarily, such calls and spontaneous outbursts of song, in this case from a caller who was both a namesake and an acquaintance of the guest-hunter, are welcome moments of extempore plot in the televised performance; the host of the programme would ordinarily take advantage of the call to join the call-and-response and flesh out the narrative. In this case, however, the host and his team simply exchanged understanding glances and kept silent. This is one rather obvious instance of the disconnect resulting from two divergent definitions of what is 'appropriate'. A similar disparity informs Babalola's choice of data. The official definition of appropriate behaviour can become so influential as to moderate the language employed in the exchange between the observer/researcher and the observed/informant. Many informants and respondents who are already apprehensive of the reigning sensibility readily 'tune' themselves to the language privileged by the researcher.

Spirituality represents another site in which praxis challenges the tidy assumptions of theory. I use 'spirituality', not 'religion', because the latter minimises the complexity of many African cosmologies. Àjùwọn's (1980:66) 'The preservation of Yoruba tradition,' has an undercurrent of the Muslim/Christian-versus-the-traditional dichotomy:

> With the arrival of Christian missionaries in 1843, the performance of the *ìrèmọ̀jé* ritual, and other Yoruba traditional practices such as ancestor worship, came under serious attack. As a result of the counter-pressure of Islam, these attacks intensified, as adherents of both religious faiths mounted a vigorous offensive against the observance of traditional Yoruba rituals and religion, considered to be 'heathen' and 'unholy' . . . In spite of persistent attacks, die-hard bearers of the Yoruba traditional religion and its rituals survived.

Admittedly, Islam and Christianity have, to a large extent, had a corrosive impact on indigenous cultural practices, but the hunter rarely, if ever, finds himself in the kind of opposition drawn by Àjùwọn. He immolates a dog every year to appease Ògún, and yet attends Sunday School or bears a Muslim name (see Plates 2.1 and 2.2).

Plate 2.1: Kọ́lá Tirimisiyu Akíntáyọ̀ (second from left) organises Ògún worship and festival, Òké-Àdó, Ibadan

Plate 2.2: Immolating the dog during Akíntáyọ̀'s festival

A couple of Muslim names from among the performers of the *ìrèmọ̀jé* collected by Àjùwọn (1981) himself are a testimony to this ecclectism, an eclecticism I observed in the field. On my first visit to the Balóḍẹ of Saki, I had to wait because he had gone to pray in the mosque. In a dark corner of the passage into the house, there was an assortment of guns and other metal objects, all of which were caked in blood (see Plate 2.3).

Plate 2.3: Lawal Oguntunde's Ogun shrine

Plate 2.4: The outer wall of Oguntunde's home

This was a sort of shrine where the Balóḍẹ occasionally spilt liquor and animal's blood to seek Ògún's favour. Right on the outer wall of the house was a bold inscription of his name in paint, a signal of the plurality of his spirituality: LAWAL . . . OGUNTUNDE (see Plate 2.4). The first name is Muslim, while the last name references Ògún, the Yoruba deity of hunting. It is also notable that neither of the names is a surname. They both refer directly to the same bearer. This is one notable aspect of identity formation in Oguntunde's generation and social class. They are largely uninfluenced by the tradition of adopting the name of one's father or husband as surname, introduced through Western education and Christianity.

In another example at another time and place, more than 100 kilometres away, a narrator who introduced himself as Alhaji (a Muslim title) at the beginning of his story commits himself to the guidance of Ògún as the conflict builds in the narrative:

> Orúkọ ọ mi ni Àlhájì Táníátù Akínkúnmi tí gbogbo èèyàn npè ní Akéwejẹ̀ n'ilùú Ìkirè . . . Nínú u'gbó l'óru . . . àwọn ẹmọ́ kan n jẹ oko n'bẹ̀. Mo wá ní dandan màá sá pa nínú u rẹ̀ ni alẹ́ ọjọ́ yẹn. Ìgbà a mo dé bẹ̀, àwọn ẹmọ́ yẹn, mi ì rí'kankan yìnbọn sí. Iwájú yẹn tí mo wá tọ̀ wípé kí n mọ kí ló n sẹlẹ̀, bí mo se bá ẹbọ yẹn l'ójú odò n'ìyẹn. Ẹ̀rú bàá mọ̀ kí n padà o. Mo bá ní kóómí 'hun tó bá sẹlẹ̀, n ó g'òkè odò yẹn. Ojú Ògún tó mi.

> [My name is Alhaji Táníátù Akínkúnmi, known by everybody in Ìkirè as Akéwejẹ̀ . . . In the forest, at night . . . I had planned to hunt some rodents that

were grazing that area of the forest that night. But when I got there, I could not find any animal to shoot at. It was when I moved further up that I came upon that sacrifice (of three duck's eggs in a shard). I almost decided to turn back. But I resolved to go on and cross the river to the other side, for *Ògún is my guide* (my italics).][18]

Ajuwon's studies moreover highlight how our conceptualisation and definition of cultural and performance forms continue to be regulated by Western typology. The awareness of such well-known Western forms as the dirge, epic and folktale seems to mobilise research primarily intended to demonstrate their African analogues. What is more, many types lack specific normative identification, even in indigenous terms. For example, the rich cultures of joke, innuendo, oath and cursing in Yoruba pervade many areas of communication, but have not received as much attention as, for example, folktale and dance. The culture of joke, for instance, not only among the Yoruba but in cosmopolitan Nigeria, eluded attention until a more formalised outgrowth of it, 'stand-up comedy', showed up at the turn of last century.

While responding to Awoonor's (1975:83) comment that 'within *Ìjálá* . . . the dirge may occur', Àjùwòn (1982:12) notes that:

This statement is somewhat misleading and should be put right. Ìjálá is the Yoruba hunters' song used either for the worship of the god Ògún, or for entertainment at occasions not specifically connected with Ògún or with hunters, such as weddings or naming of children. Dirges deal mainly with grief, morning [sic], death and loss. During the performance of ìjálá, whether for the worship of Ògún or for entertainment, dirges are not supposed to be chanted. Perhaps Kofi Awoonor has in mind ìrèmòjé, the Yoruba hunters' funeral dirges. Rather than consider dirges as ìjálá, it would be more correct to note that dirges may contain ìjálá traits such as humour.

The above statement is significant in two ways. First, it shows how an over-reliance on privileged Western typology – the dirge, epic, ballad, and so on – confuses attempt to fully appreciate indigenous forms. Second, the fact that some available *ìjálá* texts upset Àjùwòn's model – as shall be shown presently – further shows that the hunter defies boundaries.

In his preliminary examination of the dirge form, Àjùwòn appropriately reviews a similar practice among not only African peoples but also in Western cultures like Greece, Russia and Ireland. He then observes that [funeral] dirges or laments for the dead are an important genre of folklore. Dirges can be viewed as poems of lamentation which may be improvised by the mourners, according to the traditional formulae and themes' (Àjùwòn 1982:1). It is the appropriation of this definition of dirge in Àjùwòn's description of, and differentiation between, *ìrèmòjé* and *ìjálá* that defines Àjùwòn's response to Awoonor. Àjùwòn (1982:83) maintains that though *ìrèmòjé*, identified as a dirge, 'contain[s] *ìjálá* traits', 'dirges are not supposed to be chanted in *ìjálá*'. Dirges chanted as *ìjálá*, Àjùwòn holds, are a preserve of *ìrèmòjé*. But Àjùwòn's clarification is not without its pitfalls. Granted, ìrèmòjé is principally performed on the occasion of a hunter's funeral, but the obverse situation is not necessarily the case: mourning and lamentation are hardly alien to *ìjálá*. Various texts and contexts of performance of *ìjálá* show that if Àjùwòn's typology had ever been valid, it is no longer so.

Two examples will suffice. In his *ìjálá* record, *Ìgbáládùn Tabétabé*, Fóyánmu, the *ìjálá* artist, briefly recalls the death of his back-up performer, Dàpò Ìṣòlá, with grief. Apart from the poet's voice, modulated to a mournful pitch, he specifically instructs that drumming be lowered to highlight the solemnity of the dirge:

> *Mò nbò wá ná, ẹ rọra sinmi ìlù díè*
> *Ẹ ló ọ n'tínrín, ẹ tèé mólè*
> *Kó rọra máa ró, ẹ má jẹ n mò pé 'lù ni.*
>
> [Excuse me, relax the drumming a little
> Squeeze it [the drum thongs], lower the volume,
> Let the sound be faint, don't give me the impression that drumming is going on][19]

Early in 2007, Olú Atóyèbí, a radio presenter who was of the hunters' lineage, died. Akíntáyò, the host of *Ọdẹ Akọni* and a hunter and friend of Atóyèbí, spent more than five minutes of his next programme performing *ìjálá*, lamenting his friend's death. Obviously, both performances were *ìjálá*, not *ìrèmòjé*, given not only the contexts of their performance but also the fact that themes of death and mourning are not the only preoccupation.

As the examples of the hunters' narratives show on the one hand, art inheres in informal communication such as conversation. On the other hand, the attempts to formally apprehend existing identifiable forms, such as the *ìjálá* and *ìrèmòjé*, sometimes overlook agency as a determinative. The hunter – a visionary, a seeker and a 'licensed' subversive among the Yoruba – provides us a consummate illustration of the need not only to look beyond nominal categories for arts but to also reassess continually our definition and understanding of culture.

Conceptualising narrativity between fact and fiction

Taking a step back from the specific cultural instantiations of hunters' performance, we face the more general problem of the narratives' relationship to reality. For much of the twentieth century, researchers studying African culture have portrayed it as a story-telling culture, drawing primarily from a fabulous worldview. This is, again, primarily a structuralist attitude that assumes that the world can be easily divided up into categories of reality and myth, sacred and secular. It is also an entirely inappropriate way to understand Yoruba hunters' narratives.

The earliest, and most influential, writer to take this attitude was Malinowski (1922/1948), whose study of storytelling among the Tobriand Islanders identifies three basic types of narratives, namely, *kuwanebu* [fairy tales], *libwogo* [legend] and *liuliu* [myths]. About 39 years later, William Bascom (1965:3) drew generously on Malinowski's category in proposing 'prose narrative' as 'an appropriate term for the widespread and important category of verbal art which includes myths, legends and folktales'. Bascom (1965:4) defines folktales as 'prose narratives which are regarded as fiction', myths as 'prose narratives which . . . are considered to be truthful accounts of what happened in the remote past', and legend as 'prose narratives . . . which are regarded as true by the narrator and his audience' and 'set in a period considered less remote'. He cites examples from the Pacific, from among the Yoruba, the Ashanti, the Kimbundu, and the Fulani. According to Bascom (1965:11), the 'Yoruba recognise two classes of tales: folktales (*àlọ́*) and myth-legends (*ìtàn*)'. The myth-legends, Bascom continues, are 'histories' and 'regarded as historically true' in contrast to the fictional *àlọ́* [folktale]. Recognising the limitations of his definitions, he acknowledges that his description does not cover the less formal types like 'jokes or jest' and 'anecdotes' (Bascom 1965:5). Moreover, he acknowledges that the categories somewhat overlap, so much so that he combines 'myth' and 'legend' as a single type, 'myth-legend', from the outset. Later, Bascom suggests replacing the term 'folklore' with 'verbal art'. Looking through the growing studies in folklore, exemplified by the works of Alan Dundes, Richard M. Dorson and Dell Hymes, Bascom (1965:379) considers this term more suitable because of the preponderance of marginal urban forms like 'autograph book verse, automobile names, flyleaf rhymes . . ., latrinalia and traditional letters', then enjoying increasing attention in the Americas.

Despite his laudable restraint, Bascom's categories are still too sweeping to offer a comprehensive understanding of Yoruba narrative forms. If Bascom is right in his definition of *àlọ́* as fiction, the opposition to it sought in the representation of *ìtàn* is inadequate. Except when employed for academic convenience, as Bascom has done, the Yoruba do not use the term *ìtàn* in contradistinction to the fictional *àlọ́*. In fact, *ìtàn* as a label may in certain contexts subsume *àlọ́*. As such, the *àlọ́* on the exploit of the tortoise and the pig could either be referred to as '*Àlọ́ ìjàpá àti ẹlẹ́dẹ̀*' [The *àlọ́* of the tortoise and the pig] or '*Ìtàn ìjàpá àti ẹlẹ́dẹ̀*' [The *ìtàn* of the tortoise and the pig]. For example, Alabi Ogundepo, in his *ìjálá* record, *Ènìyàn ṣòro*, boasts of his qualifications as a custodian of *ìtàn* before going on to prove this by narrating an *àló* about the farmer and the ungrateful snake. Similarly, Olayemi (1969) in his paper on the *àló* uses the two terms interchangeably.

Bascom's observation on the characterisation, setting and themes of 'myth', 'legend' and 'folktale' does not reflect the Yoruba epistemology on which his study partly relies. The positivist foundation of his taxonomy is obvious in the description of setting and characterisation of 'myth', 'legend' and 'folktale'. Myth, held as factual, belongs in the remote past and is characterised by non-human principal actors. Legend, set in the recent past and contemporary world, for Bascom, also belongs in realm of fact and has only human principal characters. Folktale, the only narrative type with the potential of both human and non-human principal characters, is categorised in Bascom's (1965:5) model as 'fiction'. As such, a narrative about rodents in American shirts or antelopes turning into Fulani women and back into antelopes, is, in his reckoning, either an artefact or outright fiction.

Finnegan's (1970) *Oral Literature in Africa* raises additional issues that have animated the discourse in culture and performance through the present. In the two chapters entitled 'Prose narratives', Finnegan reviews existing interpretive models of African oral narrative forms. In her consideration of the reigning terms 'myth' and 'legend', Finnegan retains Bascom's category. However, she reflects that myth, as conceived by Bascom, might be conceptually incongruous. Finnegan (1970:332) describes her difficulties with classification during her own field experience:

> When I first heard a Limba story about how in the old days Kanu (God) lived with mankind but then withdrew in impatience to the sky, I at first automatically classed this in my mind as 'myth'. It was easy to see its function (explaining and justifying present state of things) and, like other 'myths', it was presumably well known and taken seriously . . . It was only after recording several dozen more Limba stories that I realised that this particular story was no different in style, outlook or occasion of telling from the clearly 'fictional' and light-hearted narratives about, say, a man wooing a wife or a cat plotting to eat a group of rats.

What upset Finnegan's earlier conception was the overlap of elements hitherto taken for granted as a preserve of either fantasy or realism. Later findings would reveal to her that 'there are . . . societies in which the distinction between 'myth' and 'folktale' is not observed' (Finnegan 1970:328).

The positivist fact/fiction conceptual dichotomy has influenced the assessment of African narratives for a long time. The established categories of such types as myth, legend, novel and biography, with all that their cognate characteristics imply about reality, seem to have predisposed us to categorising all forms of narratives in these shorthand terms. Bamgbose (1974:9) writes that in Fagunwa's novels, 'the world portrayed . . . is a romanticised world of kings, princes and princesses, jewelry and treasures . . . that is typically fictional and only rarely true of real life' and 'mere fantasies because of the preponderance of unusual and unlikely incidents which they contain' (1974:83). We should recall that Fagunwa's narratives exploit the infrastructure of the Yoruba hunter's point of view. Even when the protagonist-narrator is not a hunter, as in Ìrèké Oníbùdó and Àdìítú Olódùmarè, the terrains he explores are fraught with the weird and the supernatural, as are the hunter's many bushes and forests. Bamgbose (1974:84–85) later adds a caveat that

> the Yoruba believe in the world of the spirits, witches, magic and communication with the dead. A lot of the weirdness in the novels is reflection of the world view [sic]. Thus characters like àròní, the one-legged fairy, and egbére, a short creature who always sheds tears, which are found in Ògbójú are not merely fictional characters but spirits believed by the Yoruba to exist in the forest . . . For those for whom Fagunwa was writing and who basically share this world view [sic], these aspects of the novels are realistic at the level of the reader's consciousness of his world.

But apart from Bamgbose's failure to resolve the contradiction emergent from these two diametrically opposed positions, a corollary question arises: 'In whose terms should the world of Fagunwa's novels be considered "mere fantasies" and "romanticised"?' If by fantasy and romanticity, Bamgbose means the mythmaking that is characteristic not only of all the prose fiction in the Western realistic mode, but also historiography, the contradiction is resolved. But if these terms are conceived as something totally outside reality – which Bamgbose seems most likely to mean – they misrepresent the worldview that provides the background to Fagunwa's art. While admitting that what Fagunwa distils from this world of the 'unusual and unlikely' is fiction, and that he takes his materials from very catholic sources, a traditional Yoruba mind sees little or no dividing line between Fagunwa's fictional world and his/her world, a world whose weird and untamed side is sometimes pacified through the hunter. In fact, as Soyinka (2006) has rightly noted, Fagunwa himself is not spared as a character in conversational narratives composed in the mode of his fiction. One such popular narrative recounts Fagunwa's compact with the water spirit to allow him access to the supernatural narrative muse, in return for which he would give his life at an appointed time. Fagunwa's subsequent death by drowning and the rumoured disappearance of his body only further promotes this theory.[20]

In *Myth in Africa: A Study of its Aesthetic and Cultural Relevance*, Okpewho (1983), trying to redefine the concept of myth, critiques the definitions of earlier writers, like James Frazer, Carl Wilhelm von Sydow, Bronislaw Malinowski, Claude Levi-Strauss, Andre Jolles and William Bascom. All of these writers share the popular conceptualisation of myth as a narrative form, although they diverge on such issues as the function of myth, and on whether myth or ritual is the causal partner in the pair. Malinowski (1998:176) suggests that myth has a plastic narrative quality, and that, by inference, the performativity of myth is therefore determined by the expertise of the narrator:

> [Myth] has its literary aspect – an aspect which has been unduly emphasised by most scholars, but which, nevertheless, should not be completely neglected. Myth contains the germs of the future epic, romance, and tragedy; and it has been used in them by the creative genius of peoples and by conscious art of civilisation.

In Malinowki's view (1998:176), myth therefore 'lends itself in certain of its forms to subsequent literary elaboration'. This observation is essentially identical with the maxim credited to Joseph Fotenrose: 'no story, no myth' (Okpewho 1983:48). Levi-Strauss, the structuralist theoretician and one of the writers critiqued by Okpewho (1983:104), reflects that myth 'is language, functioning on an especially high level where meaning succeeds practically at "taking off" from the linguistic ground on which it keeps on rolling'. Levi-Strauss's comments here pertain to the aspect of mythical imagination that challenges our normative way of seeing; the normative sensibility labelled by Rabkin (1977:10) as the 'armchair worldview'.

Okpewho (1983:69) rejects one aspect of the existing definitions of myth that conceptualises it as an identifiable narrative form, and as a corrective, he offers that:

> Myth is not really a particular type of tale against another . . . It is simply that quality of fancy which informs the creative or configurative powers of the human mind in varying degrees of intensity. In that sense, we are free to call any narrative of the oral tradition a myth, so long as it gives emphasis to fanciful play.

Okpewho thereby appropriates the aggregate description of some of the earlier writers who presume that myth has the capacity for redefining ordinary 'everyday' reality. It is this aspect of myth that Malinowski advises that students of culture approach with humility. Locating a dividing line between historical reality and fictive 'fancy' is inadequate if it superimposes a totally different conceptual grid on the worldview under study. This is where the weakness of Okpewho's study lies. The weakness is not in his lack of confidence in the narrator as a bearer of total truth; no storyteller of whatever genre is expected to be a 'truth-teller' in the absolute sense anyway. The weakness lies in his counsel that the researcher should 'be bold enough to assume *an objective distance* and . . . recognise an honest line between what is lifelike and what is not' (Okpewho 1983:6 [my italics]). It is the kind of 'objective distance' advised by Okpewho that inspires what Yai (1999: 32) terms 'intransitive discourses', an attitude that largely disregards the views of the people about their own worldview and cultural practices.

Bascom (1965:7) writes that 'the distinction between fact and fiction refers . . . to the belief of those who tell and hear these tales and not to our beliefs, to historical or scientific laws, or any ultimate judgment of truth or falsehood'. Levi-Strauss (1998), more daringly, argues that myth straddles the thresholds of fact and fiction; it is futile therefore to locate it specifically in the historical or physical plane. Levi-Strauss further insists that the constituent elements of myths, which he refers to as 'mythemes' elsewhere, may not also be classified as exactly historical or fictional. These theses – those of Bascom, Levi-Strauss and others – have their own problems, many of which, today, are well-advertised not only in the discourses on the arts, but also in sociology. But Okpewho's reason for rejecting them is faulty. His rejection carries with it some of the colonial anthropologist's complex that presumes to regard the 'object' of study from a higher realm of awareness; a complex premised on the assumption that 'the researcher should know better':

> We therefore need a new approach, and I suggest a qualitative one . . . By this I mean that we have to qualify every tale – whether in prose or verse, whatever the distinction means; whether in a sacred or secular environment; in whatever manner or belief it is held in its indigenous setting – on the basis of our own scientific recognition of the relative weight of fact and fiction in it (Okpewho 1979:59).

Literary critic Rabkin (1977) reasons that the 'fantastic' conceived as antonymous to the 'realistic' is often a product of intellectual weakness. This is especially so when the observer is either ignorant of or unwilling to accept the 'ground rules' through which the so-called fantastic is considered a reality. Indeed, language has the potential to heighten the sense of the fantastic if the observer is innocent of its ground rules. Using structuralist schema, he points out that a grammar (*langue*) and an individual performance (*parole*) are predetermined by sets of rules that may not necessarily correspond: aberration in the observer's terms might be adherence for the user of language under study. It is the lazy reluctance to experience the 'ground rules' which legitimises such 'aberration' that often leads to the classification of the narratives employing the 'aberrant' medium as 'escape' – as opposed to 'serious' – art. According to Rabkin (1977:44), 'this is a pernicious dichotomy that derives from two misconceptions: first, that 'seriousness' is better than 'escape'; second, that escape is an indiscriminate rejection of order'. Therefore, it is needless to labour to reconfigure cultural idioms to fit into the expressive system supported by the external observer's hegemony. It is not absurd to affirm alterity: the Other and the Self do 'experience different realities, not simply the same realities in different ways' (Rabkin 1977:77).

Motz (1998:340) traces the root of the Western positivist tradition that considers *belief* – 'a process of knowing that is not subject to verification or measurement by experimental means within the framework of a modern Western scientific paradigm' – to the nineteenth-century industrial revolution. It was one aspect of the technocentric bias of the time to consider the domestic side of life as less important to the place of work and machines. This attitude, Motz argues citing Michel de Certeau, survives in the form of popular research and academic practice in which traditional knowledge and practices are labeled 'folkways' and held to be subordinate or outright inferior to the physical sciences. Building on the observation of Jean-Francois Lyotard, Motz (1998:343) writes that although traditional ways of knowing are 'judged by criteria developed through consensus within a community and extend beyond the cognitive assessment of truth', they nevertheless do not foreclose the legitimacy of the Western modern scientific knowledge. But Western science, long adapted to the truth/falsity dichotomy, rejects traditional knowledge. This 'scientific' refusal to know is apprehended here as a limitation; a limitation that traditional knowledge has surmounted because it acknowledges scientific knowledge. But the traditional modes of perception and expression do not only survive in the technocentric world, they in fact enjoy renewal through such cultural practices as rituals, narratives and songs that not only perpetuate them but also stimulate belief in them.

Hemminger (2001) also eloquently explains the rationality in the belief in the spiritual as a realm of reality. In his reading of Okri – a writer who uses themes, characters and settings similar to those used by the hunter-narrator – Hemminger adopts the postulation of Martin Heidegger to interrogate the positivist anthropocentric disregard and denial of the world of objects. It should be noted that Heidegger's thought departs from the philosophical mainstream of his time in its elastic conceptualisation of *Dasein* – 'being-in-the-world' – to include objects and realities that are not accessible to the mundane senses. For Hemminger, as for Heidegger, the denial of the alternative reality of the spirit world is not just sin but atrophy, for the positivist who fails to recognise the spiritual as an authentic dimension of existence denies himself relation with this reality and additionally blunts his own potential for sensing it. Hemminger asserts that for the people for whom Okri (2001:67) writes, 'the world of spirits is not metaphorical or imaginary; rather, it is more real than the world of the everyday'. But for a mind attuned to positivism to retain a vision of the spiritual requires keen circumspection. Hemminger (2001:79) points out Azaro, a principal character in Okri's novels, as a validation of this:

> Azaro has foreknowledge though he makes a terrible student; in a comic way, his inaptitude for school programs that so strongly stress cognitive operations and verbal skills becomes a criticism of our own academic programs, which sacrifice intrapersonal development or musical thinking or kinesthetic intelligence for programs that valorise logico-mathematic thinking.

In an article entitled 'What people like us are saying when we say we're saying the truth', Jackson (1988) problematises the kind of 'scientific recognition' of 'fact and fiction' pursued by Okpewho. Man, according to Jackson (1988:380), survives on storytelling: 'Stories are the way we manage reality for ourselves and our presentation of ourselves to others.' But the need to present the story in a manner 'acceptable' because it is 'beautiful' does threaten the 'truth' in the absolute sense. Jackson (1988:282) therefore acknowledges 'the ability of narrators to skirt the intentional and moral character of events without uttering anything that might be a literal untruth'. Using the example of Pete McKenzie, an American convict on the death row for ten years who avoids execution 'by being declared legally insane,' he argues that man may use 'the storyteller's art to make the past reasonable and bearable and manageable'. In such a situation, he 'wasn't lying, but he wasn't telling the truth either' (Jackson 1988:280). This is the point where language, as Rabkin also agrees, goes beyond being a medium of a message to becoming a part of it: 'Diction is a component of substance, not vehicle for it' (Jackson 1988:282). But beyond recognising the narrator's intention in the process of mythmaking, Jackson (1988:283) asserts that the prevalence of uncertainty at the heart of the twentieth-century human life, including uncertainty in the physical sciences, has considerably redefined the boundary between fact and fiction. Uncertainty has reduced the veracity of scientific prediction: 'Uncertainty has to do with a limitation of our ability to know; ambiguity has to do with a multiplicity of meaning extant at once and without contradiction or cancellation.'

The immanence of uncertainty that became palpable for Westerners only in the twentieth century had, for the Yoruba, been a primordial awareness, as illustrated in the quest for the understanding of ambiguated reality sought through the hunter's eye. Even in his genuine intention to capture the scientific truth, man is handicapped, his microphone and lens notwithstanding. Reflecting on his experience in the field, Jackson (1988:285) observes that time and the sensible need to take out the 'representative' examples for presentations downplay 'the infinitude of information'. This is why the so-called factual field report can never attain the height of 'the whole truth': 'You see only what they made. If you want to see what they see, go with them next time' (Jackson 1988:288).

Having considered some observations on the nature of reality and belief, narrativity and the impossibility of absolute truth, and myth, this study adopts a working definition of myth that combines select strands from some of them. Okpewho's definition of myth is adopted in its sense as a narrative quality, not necessarily as a narrative form. It is, in fact, in the apprehension of myth as a quality in the narrative process that the term 'mythmaking', rather than 'myth', is often employed to underline the performativity in which it is manifest. However, the challenge of separating 'fanciful play' from 'fact' that Okpewho advises is only surmountable at the cost of subjectivity. Living hunters relate experiences replete with events that qualify immediately, using Okpewho's parameters, as 'fanciful play'. But the hunter and many of his listeners hold them as true as the palm of the hand. I do not therefore intend to determine either the actuality or fictionality of a narrative by virtue of its 'life size' or weird events and characterisation. I admit, however, that fictionality is an aspect of the hunter's narrative, as it is of any human attempt to relive the past. Mythmaking as conceived here is therefore the sum discrepancy between the event *of* the narrative and the event *in* the narrative. It is the essential human selection, through exclusion and inclusion, of events in the process of narrative performance. Instances of contradiction in a narrative performance, or in different versions of a narrative performance, serve to instantiate mythmaking as an essential aspect of narrative performance.

The hunter's way continually veers off the conventional path. Even in the performance of such arts as *ìjálá* and *ìrèmòjé* that are considered formalised, his non-conformist temper is noticeable in how he wilfully negates and reinvents terms of performance in manners that are different from the known order. At the level of formalised forms, such as *ìjálá* and *ìrèmòjé*, the hunter merely reflects the cultural propensity for upsetting and reinventing terms as do the performers of *èsà* and *ìyèrè*. But as he is an innovative performer of *ìjálá*, the Yoruba hunter's intractable temperament situates him in the forefront of not just continuity but also subversive regeneration of the culture he inherited. Particularly, his knowledge of, and familiarisation with the wild and the supernatural reflect the Yoruba understanding of them, and also generate new modes of understanding and relation. It is ultimately in the narrative reconstruction of real-life experience that the Yoruba hunter noticeably breaks through the cordons of definition of not only art, but of reality.

Notes

1. *Ọdẹ Akọni*, 03/06/2007.

2. Ìdọ̀ha and Ìlàrẹ́ are mythical towns, home to each of the *babaláwo*.

3. *Ọdẹ Akọni*, 01/08/04.

4. Personal interaction, 07/10/2007.

5. *Ọdẹ Akọni*, 13/06/04.

6. Personal interaction, 20/11/2005.

7. Personal interaction, 11/02/2007.

8. *Ọdẹ Akọni*, 20/02/2005.

9. *Ọdẹ Akọni*, 12/09/2004.

10. Bead used as pectoral adornment by Ṣàngó worshippers.

11. Personal interaction, 11/02/2007.

12. *Ọdẹ Akọni*, 12/09/2004.

13. *Chlorophora excelsa.*

14. *Ọdẹ̀tẹ̀dó*, n.d.

15. An archdeity.

16. *Oríkì orílẹ̀* of the *Òbùro* lineage, Ìsẹ̀kẹ́, Ọ̀yọ́, Oyo State.

17. *Ọdẹtẹdo*, n.d.

18. *Ọdẹ Akọni*, 24/12/2006.

19. *Ìgbáládùn Tabẹ́tabẹ́*, n.d.

20. One such narrator is Mrs Aderoju Adeduntan of Ṣakí, a school teacher.

3

The Hunter and the Other

Introduction

As pursued in Chapter 2, the Yoruba hunter's perception does not support the reigning epistemological partitioning of narratives into reality and fiction on the basis of their weird and uncanny contents. Furthermore, I argue that the tradition of perceiving the world solely in such opposite terms, as shown in works in philosophy and cultural studies, is informed by the dualist orientation with which Western philosophy has infected our conceptualisation. The orientation reaches as far as the structuralist mode of understanding which not only reaffirms the immanence of opposites but also privileges the positivist sentiments, especially the one that subordinates the supernatural as an order of reality.

Dualism, African cultural discourse, and the hunter

For the better part of the twentieth century, indigenous African scholars and Europeans, some of them missionaries, attempted to interrogate the Hegelian notion that African thought and cultural practices are sites of innocence, simplicity and savagery. But even sympathetic attempts to interpret African culture have struggled with notions of hierarchy, particularly in teasing out the borders between the animate and the inanimate. The hunter's narrative offers both an illustration of this difficulty and a lens through which to develop a more sophisticated understanding of Yoruba cosmology.

One early attempt to provide an understanding of African epistemology was Tempels' *Bantu philosophy* (1959). In his observation of the Luba people of Congo, Tempels posits that the people's perception of their world includes an inherent philosophy. In Tempels' reckoning, the concepts of 'being' and 'force' are central to Bantu ontology, and he (1959:50–51) calls attention to the inseparability of these two entities as opposed to the reigning Western dualist thinking:

> We [Europeans] can conceive the transcendental notion of 'being' by separating it from its attribute, 'force', but the Bantu cannot. 'Force' in his thought is a necessary element in 'being', and the concept 'force' is

inseparable from the definition of 'being'. There is no idea among Bantu of 'being' divorced from the idea of 'force'.

Beings, whether human, divine, animal or vegetal, operate within a principle termed 'general laws of vital causality'. In this system, a being, by virtue of the strength of its force, can either harvest more strength from another being, or, in contrast, lose some strength to a stronger being. Man as a being, for example, can either strengthen or weaken the being of another man; the being of man can also affect the subordinate being of animal or plant.

Tempels' daring in challenging the very Hegelian episteme that provided the basis for the colonialist and missionary incursion is widely acknowledged (Jahn 1961; Kagame 1956; Mudimbe 1988). But his thesis, as did many others that followed, contains a holdover of the idea that the classical/Western tradition is a higher order of knowledge. Tempels (1959:36) states unequivocally that Bantu thought, still inchoate, needs to be conceptualised in Western terms to become philosophy in the explicit sense: 'It is *our* job to proceed to such systematic development. It is *we* who will be able to tell *them* in precise terms, what *their* inmost concept of being is' [my italics].

Moreover, as p'Bitek (1973), the Ugandan poet, has argued, Tempels assumes that Bantu ontology is essentially representative of African traditional thought, and Tempels' conception of Bantu ontology has itself been subject to criticism. Kagame (1956), for example, contends that Tempels' representation of Bantu ontology is distorted by the foreign idiom he employed. Kagame writes, for instance, that although examples of universal parallels abound in the Bantu linguistic system, Tempels' consideration of 'being' and 'force' as identifiable units is odd.

Even the cosmological hierarchy implicit in Tempels' 'general laws of vital causality' is problematic. The laws suggest that a rational being, represented by man or spirit, is above animals, plants and other natural objects. The exclusive attribution of rationality, and therefore superiority, to a class identified as either 'man' or 'spirit' distorts many cultural representations. A culture like the Yoruba, for example, does not operate under such a neat hierarchy in which a rational 'being' stands in contradistinction to the 'irrational' and 'inanimate.' As can be inferred from the hunters' narratives, the ontological estates that would ordinarily be considered either animate or inanimate overlap in Yoruba culture. As such, a forest or a tree may be hostile in a very literal sense, or the whirlwind may try to kidnap the hunter. Moreover, Yoruba hunters do not always act in a subordinate-versus-superordinate system, but rather sometimes participate in symbiosis and compromise.

African scholars, too, are prone to generalisations and conceptualisations influenced by Western tradition. Two of Idowu's works (*Olodumare* and *African traditional religion*), for example, attempt a description of African cosmology using the dualist interpretive grid (Bewaji 1999; Wiredu 1998). Idowu's work is largely aimed at demonstrating that the African conception of God and deities is analogous to the Western type, and therefore not inferior to it. The result is that religious and cultural elements are rationalised to show their similarity with Christianity. Idowu objects to the misconception that Yoruba culture is essentially animist, arguing that the misnomer 'animism' stems from the foreign investigator's mistake of assuming that Africans regard natural objects as living rational entities. According to Idowu (1973:173), the African worldview is instead hinged on

> a belief in, recognition and acceptance of the fact of the existence of spirits who may use material objects as temporary residences and manifest their presence and actions through natural objects and phenomena.

Idowu is right up to a point. There is one sense in which a material phenomenon or an object is seen as mere habitation of a spirit, as there is another in which the spirit and the object in which it resides are seen as one and the same. But in the effort to totally debunk the animist theory, there is a risk of creating a dualist formation that somewhat undercuts the vitality of the intercourse – or the conjunction – of matter and spirit. The Yoruba, one of the principal foci of Idowu's studies, do not, for example, sometimes conceive of spirit and the object with which it is associated as separable. In a manner of speaking, a rock or a river might be conceived in the hunter's narrative as the owner of the entire population of animals in a particular forest. This does not mean that every tree or rock in the forest is thought of in such terms, but it does imply that the spirits and the natural objects through which the spirits are manifest are seen as conjoined as are man and his life. The hunter Táníátù Akéwejẹ̀ holds a rock and an àràbà tree[1] responsible for the disappearance of the deer he shot earlier. He issues them both an ultimatum:

> Ìwọ àpáta àti àràbà, ìwọ lo gbàbọ̀dè o. T'óo bá kọ̀ láti má gbé ẹran yìí jáde láàrin àsìkò táa wa nbi'i, o 'ò níí r'éwé b'orí mọ́ o.

> [You the rock and the àràbà tree have conspired to shield the animal. If you fail to produce it within the time of my stay in this forest, there will be no single leaf left on you as shade and protection.][2]

The àràbà tree and the rock, on the one hand, and whatever spirit they harbour on the other, are considered therefore as one. It is instructive to recall that the death or eviction of such a spirit is often marked by the atrophy of the tree.

Mbiti replays, on a larger scale, Idowu's reductionism. He states that 'the African view of the universe is profoundly religious' (Mbiti 1975:32), and locates man at the centre of creation. According to Mbiti (1975:38), because 'man thinks of himself as being the centre [of the universe], he consequently sees the universe from that perspective. It is as if the world exists for man's sake'. Following a premise that 'even where there is no biological life in an object, the African peoples attribute (mystical) life to it', Mbiti (1975) writes that such a belief is now only extant in rural communities, and will soon be out of fashion with the spread of 'scientific ideas'. Later on, with the aid of a diagram, he tidily categorises spirits into 'nature spirits' and 'human spirits'. Nature spirits are further divided into 'sky spirits' and 'earth spirits,' and the human spirits into 'long dead' and 'recently dead' (Mbiti 1975:65). But these definitions are surely too exact to account for the intractable nature of the spirits as conceived by the Yoruba hunters. As Mbiti himself notes in a caveat, a nature spirit might be considered as having once lived as man. In the narrative cited above, Akéwejè claims that a particular river was a hunter in his lifetime as man and, therefore, could not have denied a fellow hunter of his kill. There is additionally the potential of the so-called nature spirit getting married to man the hunter, a construct that upsets Mbiti's (1975:70) description of nature spirits as having 'no direct physical kinship with people'. Fagunwa (1950a/b) seizes upon this potential in his characterisation of Kako, a hunter of human and spirit extractions.

Babalawo and Yoruba studies scholar, Abimbola (1986) does an appraisal of Yoruba thought and cosmology, using *Ifá* as supertext, Abimbola places the Deity Olodumare at the apex of the cosmological hierarchy. In the malevolent half of the cosmological whole, superintended by Olodumare, are the *ajogun* and the *eníyán*, while *òrìsà*, *egúngún*, *orí* and *ènìyàn* occupy the benevolent half. *Èsù*, the impartial and intractable essence of Olodumare, is located in the border between these two worlds. Abimbola's malevolent/benevolent dichotomy is not entirely valid for Yoruba cosmology. If the *ajogun* are explicitly malevolent, the *eníyán* (often misrepresented as witches) are a complex of both evil and good. The *eníyán* or *àjé*, as can be inferred from a number of traditional performance texts, are latent with multivalent capacities, as are the *òrìsà* that Abimbola situates in the benevolent class (Adeduntan 2008). It is obvious that *ènìyàn*, man, called benevolent in Abimbola's classification, is the most indeterminate of all. Lastly, the spirits, sometimes designated as *òrò*[3] in *odù* of *Ifá*, are not given any specific space in Abimbola's schema.

In his essay cited above, Wiredu (1998) observes among writers on African thought, religion and culture, the apologetic tendency to redefine African epistemology to suit Western privileged sensibilities and models. Dualist conceptualisations of African epistemology by philosophers of the scholastic genre – many of them African – are an example of this influence. Instead, he suggests 'particularistic studies' as a remedial approach that examines each culture or cultural site individually, without unnecessarily superimposing explanations composed from other cultures. Wiredu has been particularly active in questioning the implicit and explicit assumption that African cosmology is dualist, as indicated by his debates with other scholars, some conducted through private correspondence. It is important to quote at length the aspect of Wiredu's (1998:Par 60) thesis that generated the debate and correspondence:

> The beings I have, by implication, described as superhuman (but, note, not supernatural) are often called spirits. If the notion of spirit is understood in quasi-physical sense, as they sometimes are, in narratives of ghostly apparitions even in Western thought, there is no problem of conceptual incongruity. But if the word 'spirit' is construed, as so often happens, in a Cartesian sense to designate an immaterial substance, no such category can be fitted into the conceptual framework of the Akan thought. The fundamental reason for this is to be found in the spatial connotation of Akan concept of existence. Given the necessary spatiality of all existents, little reflection is required to see that the absolute ontological cleavage between the material and the immaterial will not exist in Akan metaphysics. Again, that Africans are said to believe in spiritual entities in the immaterial sense can be ascribed to the conceptual impositions in the accounts of African thought during colonial times and their post-colonial aftermath.

His correspondent, African scholar of metaphysics, Gbadegesin (1998) insists on the dualist dichotomy, maintaining that spirits occupy the immaterial realm since even those who commune with them have to acquire a special facility to do so. In response, Wiredu (quoted in Gbadegesin 1998:159) argues further that 'the concept of seeing is bound up with spatiality' and that '[however] heightened the powers of an eye may become, if it *sees* something, that thing will have to be in space'. Gbadegesin (1998:159) insists on the positivist dichotomy, that whatever is conceived through the primed third eye of the 'herbalist' – and the hunter, of course – 'cannot be taken as evidence of a physical existence of the sighted beings'.

Yet for the Yoruba hunter, such as Moses Ògúnwálé, who recounts his seven-day ordeals at the hands of the subterranean midget spirits, no such dichotomy exists. That is what the *àdó* and *atọ́* memorabilia he took from the spirits and displays are meant to underline (see Plates 3.1 and 3.2; Chapter 4).

Plate 3.1: Moses Ògúnwálé displays his memorabilia

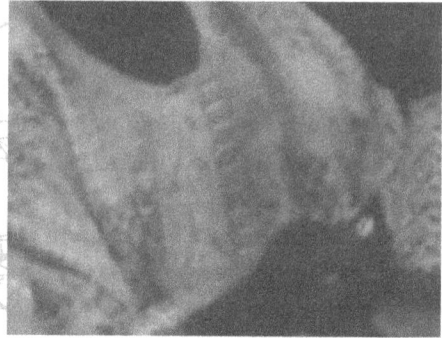

Plate 3.2: Ásìmíyù Ògúndépò Pabíẹkùn shows the gourdlet the spirit gave him

Or consider an incident from nearly half a century ago. In 1948, Nigerian writer Amos Tutuola wrote to Focal Press, asking 'if Focal Press would like to consider a manuscript about spirits in the Nigerian bush illustrated with the photographs of the spirits!' (Lindfors 1999:110–111). Whether Tutuola could later persuade the spirits to pose for photographs or not is not the issue here – rather it is the inference that the writer has allotted them space in the same reality inhabited by the photogenic mundane that is of interest.

As the Yoruba hunter sees it, being is not clearly divisible into spirit and matter. Despite that, the Yoruba worldview, as affirmed and interrogated by the hunter, does not explicitly discount the existence of a life force that drive man, animal, plant and other beings, it does not envisage a neat cleavage of that force from the body it inhabits. The conceptual incongruity begins from the adoption of 'spirit', 'ghost', and so on, to denote entities that many African cultures consider as existential parallel of man.

Man the hunter and the supernatural

The forest, as noted by Apter (1992), is the realm of infinite possibilities. At once, it holds for those who come life, death, trophy and atrophy. For humans, the forest is immediately perceived as an agonistic half of man's world. The hunter, through whom man explores and defines the unknown, sometimes starts to describe his role as agent of pacification through the very name he assumes. Performance studies scholar Layiwola (1993) considers the portrait of the hunter-characters in Fagunwa's *Ogbójú ọdẹ nínú Igbó Irúnmalẹ̀* (1950b) as illustrative of the eternal imperative to balance the 'Manichean halves' of existence. He points out that the roll-call of the major hunters mobilised for expedition to Mount Langbodo on behalf of their people immediately reveals this.

Many Yoruba hunters, in this manner of speaking, take names that define them in an agonistic relation to the unknown realm of existence they are called upon to explore. These names, called occupational pseudonyms by Izevbaye (1995), often become more popular than the hunters' original names. Músílíù Àlàgbé, a hunter from Ìwó in Ọṣun State, is thus named Fìríàáríkú [At-close-quarters-with-death]. He disclosed during an interaction:

> N náà sì ni gbogbo Ìwó mọ̀ mí sí t'ée dé Ọlá Olúwa. B'éèyàn bá bèèrè Músílíù tí wọn ọ̀ bá dáákọ Fìríàáríkú, ẹẹ̀ lè rí i.

> [That is the name all the people in Ìwó call me, even up to Oòlá Olúwa. If you identify me as Musiliu, without adding Fìríàáríkú, you might not be able to get to me.] (See Appendix A.)

Such names are common among the Yoruba hunters. They include Òkútaòtutù [He-that-is-hard-as-rock]; Ajíjààgùn [He-who-starts-the-day-by-wielding-magical-power]; Améringùn [He-who-mounts-the-elephant]; Àkámọ́ọ̀pẹkùn [Difficult-to-corner-like-the-leopard]; Àpátaárorò(-olókodáasí) [The-malevolent-rock-that-forbids-the-farmer-to-come-near-it]; Yáwọ́ọrẹ́ [He-who-is-quick-to-flog]; (Ikútíí-)Dẹ́tunhà [Death-that-breaks-the-duiker's-ribs]; Paramọ́lẹ̀(-tọ́kọ̀rọ̀ọ̀wọ̀sí) [The-viper-that-condones-no-abuse]; Pabíẹkùn [He-who-kills-like-the-leopard]; Lákátabú [The Elephant]; Amìrókò(-bíọ̀gẹ̀dẹ̀) [He-who-shakes-the-ìrókò[4]-as-if-it-were-a-mere-banana-stem]; Agbérinmì [He-who-swallows-the-elephant]; (Fàdá-)Pabíọ̀sẹ́tù [He-that-kills-with-machete-in-the-absence-of-gunpowder]; and so on.

Similarly, some of the forests are situated in a nominal class that counterbalances the hunters' names: Yaríyarí [That-which-swells-the-head]; Olójúoró [The-stern-faced-one]; Ìkookò [The Wolf]; Onígbàágó [Forest of thorns]; Ọlọ́mọ́namọ [He-that-flogs-own-child]; Ògìdán [The Leopard]; Fẹ̀jẹ̀bọ́jú [He-that-washes-face-with-blood]; and so on.

This prima facie bush-versus-homefront opposition portrays the hunter as an antagonistic quester. Since he emerges from a space that exists in contradistinction to the forest, his exploration is appreciated as a sort of incursion. In the narrative of Músílíù Àlàgbé Fìríàáríkú of Iwo (see Appendix A), the hunter explores Oníwòrò, a forest that, like Fagunwa's Olódùmarè and Irúnmalẹ̀, is notoriously peopled by malevolent supernatural beings bent on liquidating all human intruders. In an earlier version of this narrative, broadcast on Ọdẹ Akọni, the host Kọ́lá Akíntáyọ̀ evokes this sense of foreboding: 'Igbó Oníwòrò yí, ẹnìkan ìí dẹ̀ 'gbẹ́ lọọ 'bẹ̀ k'ọ́ bọ́ o. Igbó burúkú gbáà tọ́ l'ágbára gbáà ni' [No hunter goes to the Forest of Oníwòrò and returns. It is evil and indeed very malevolent].[5]

In a personal interaction about a year and a half after, Fìríàáríkú himself corroborated that '*odẹ kan ọ́ dẹ 'gbó hun kọ́ bọ̀ rí . . . Kọ̀ s'ọ́dẹ kan tí ọ́ dẹ 'gbó hun tí ọ́ bọ̀*' [no hunter ever hunted into that forest and returned . . . No hunter would go into that forest and return alive].[6] Tension builds very early in the narrative as Fìríàáríkú sets out to hunt in Oníwòrò. The hunter's adversity in the forest begins as he runs into a woman seated under a large tree. She is mute and does not respond to the hunter's greetings. Now the narrator's designation of this character, who is immediately established as an antagonist from the point when she spurns the hunter's overture, as a woman is merely nominal, for it is nigh impossible that a woman – or a man for that matter – would go unaccompanied to a forest so notorious and far away from home. Even though neither of the two narrators specifically refers to her as such, she is immediately recognised as a spirit.

If any doubts existed about the woman, they are removed as soon as the hunter returns to the spot where she sits, despite having gone away from her. On three separate occasions, the hunter attempts to leave, taking a different route in opposite directions; yet each time, he returns to the same spot. In one of the instances, he crosses a river, thereby precluding the possible theory that he must have been explicably caught in a labyrinth; he would ordinarily have had to cross the river again to get back to the woman. Upon being thus frustrated the third time, '*Mọ wáá t'ọwọ́ bọ 'kùn, mọ fà'bínú yọ*' [I put hand in my gut and brought out a fit of anger]: the hunter takes out a charm from his cloak, applies it and '*ojúù mi wáá yà*' [my eyes opened]. He thus liberates himself from the 'woman's' spell and connects to a road that leads him to Ògbògbò, near Ìjẹ̀bú-Òde: '*Bí 'ọ bá jẹ́ pé mo múra lọ́'ọ láti núu 'lé pé n'torí a 'ìi mọ̀, ah! eégún ọdẹ ọ̀ bá fẹ́ẹ̀ gbé ọ̀jẹ́ n'jọ́ náà o. Ọ dàbí nkan*' [Had I not equipped myself properly from home, *the hunter's masquerade would have perished in the grove* that day. It was a wonder].[7]

For Tàfá Àlàdé, victory is more decisive (see plates 3.3 and 3.4).[8] The hunter is on an expedition to the Forest of Olóògùn. Early in the evening, he kills two duikers and hides them before he goes further. After a moment, he starts to shiver with cold. He continues on his way, and after walking about a mile, he starts to feel so hot that he is drenched in sweat. Tàfá is, however, resolved to continue because: '*Eégún èé s'ílé wọ̀ kí wọn ọ́ nà á. 'Ọ̀nà 'ọ̀ sí ń'bẹun' ni wọn ó wìí*' [The *egungun* masquerade that misses its way is never beaten on account of that. He would rather be redirected. 'That place is no road' is what they tell him]. He later sights and shoots a huge deer, leaving it hidden somewhere after clipping its ears and tail. He then goes back to his base in the forest in order to invite his mates to help with cutting up the animal, taking with him the two duikers he killed earlier. As the hunter approaches the base, he is waylaid by a woman '*[tí]ọ́ d'aṣọ dúdú kọ́ 'rùn báyìí*' [swathed in a dark cloth], who accuses him of killing animals that do not belong to him. When the hunter tries to placate the woman, he fails and he simply *tells* her to go home and '*sinmi*' [take some rest]. Tàfá abruptly closes his story with a snappy ending: '*Ń'gbà à'yá ée wọ'lé, ìyá ti kú*' [Before she got home, she died].

Plate 3.3: Tàfá Àlàdé and audience on Ọdẹ́tẹ̀do   Plate 3.4: Tàfá Àlàdé on Ọdẹ́tẹ̀do

Akéwejè (youth leader), the occupational pseudonym of Táníátù Akínkúnmi of Ikire, Osun State, puts him in his narrative not only in the vanguard of the community as a hunter, as is traditional, but also in the very frontline of that vanguard. His portrait as the most prominent member in his hunting team is further inscribed on his gun, whose report differentiates it from other guns used by his mates. Akéwejè's first narrative is set in the Forest of Sasàá, during a group hunt called *wawàá*:

> *Igbó t'áa ma n pè ní wawàá ni tí ìkan n'nú àwọn ọmọ ọdẹ tàbí àgbà ọdẹ bá fẹ́ se ìnáwó, tó bá wáá bẹ ìgbẹ́, aá kó ajá, kó ìbọn, aá si kó àwọn èèyàn lẹyìn, aá lọ s'óko.*

> [*Wawàá* is the group hunting that we do, using dogs and guns, to help a fellow hunter, young or elderly, who is planning to celebrate an occasion source for meat.][9]

From his position during the watch, Akéwejè does not *see* but rather *perceives* that a deer is before him. That the deer stands in front of him and is not covered by the foliage guarantees that it should be visible to the hunter. But in the present case, '*kóóko ò bò ó, but mi ò rí i*' [it was not covered by the foliage, yet I did not see it]. It is with this suggestion of invisibility that the narrator first establishes the supernatural status of the antagonist. The hunter later shoots the deer and '*ọta hóró kan ò s'òfò lára a rẹ̀*' [all the bullets found their right target], yet the deer simply walks away.

The premise that Akéwejè, the protagonist, could perceive the invisible deer also establishes his capacity to sense beyond what is possible to perceive with the mundane facilities of eyes and ears. When he later converses with the river, the rock and the tree, it is in keeping with the dialogic order previously established. The protagonist leads a search for the fleeing deer to a river, wades in and asks: '*Ìwọ odò, tọ́ bá jẹ́ se pé ìwọ lọ gbàbọdè ẹran yìí, èmi ti pa á o*' [River, if you it is that shields this animal, be informed now that I have killed it]. But the hunter feels that the river could not have taken his animal in any case, since '*a 'ìí jọọ́ da 'lẹ̀ araa wa*' [the river and I had been trusted allies]. Soon afterwards, the hunter is attracted by dogs fretting around a nearby àràbà[10] tree and a rock. Upon inspection, he discovers the footprints of the animal leading to the base of the two, not away from it. The suggestion is that the animal has escaped *into* the tree and the rock. He therefore approaches the antagonist pair – àràbà and rock – with the confidence of a detective catching an offender in *flagrante delicto*:

> *Ìwọ àpáta àti àràbà, ìwọ lọ gb'àbọdè o. T'óo bá kọ̀ láti má gbé ẹran yìí jáde láàrin àsìkò t'áa wà nbì'í, oò níí r'éwé b'orí mọ́ o.*

> [You rock and àràbà tree, you are shielding a fugitive. If you do not evict the animal at this very moment, no single leaf would be left on you as shade.]

Unlike in the first monologue, the hunter describes a very identifiable battle line between himself and the àràbà-rock. He speaks with the conviction that the pair has his deer, and it will be returned to him, even if it means confrontation. Perhaps intimidated by the hunter's threat, the àràbà-rock releases the hunter's kill, but the deer is in a state of total decomposition. What is strange in the event is that a dead deer usually takes up to six days before starting to decompose. This animal, however, discovered after only three days, has decomposed so rapidly that no tissue remains.

The hunter deems the tree and rock responsible. He therefore returns to the tree and the rock with *èpè* [a malediction spell], and curses them. As the tree withers and dies at the end of the story, the hunter ultimately emerges triumphant, boasting: '*B'írin bá kan'rin ni àwọn t'án bí wa ma n wí, ìkan ọ́ tẹ̀ fún'kan*' [when two iron bars are locked in a fight, so say our fathers, the weaker gives way].

For Akéwejè, the hunter fights to the finish. Initial failure should not deter him in his exploration of the realm of the Other. In another episode of his narrative, Akéwejè confronts the Other in form of Oníkùkùté, a forest notorious for stymieing hunters. The conflict begins with the hunter encountering a ritual symbol: the hunter finds three duck's eggs in a shard. The hunter, fluent in the medium of signification of the wild, confidently concludes that the items are primed and placed there to thwart him. Duck's eggs and a shard of pottery – items from the human world – readily establish the mystery through which the narrative anchors its indictment of the forest-spirit. The hunter therefore begins the day's exercise aware that he has an antagonist to contend with – an awareness that he demonstrates as he commits himself to the guidance of Ògún, the hunter's patron deity. In this episode, the forest antagonist subdues the hunter. Akéwejè loses mental consciousness and wanders, insensate, in the bush for about two hours. He only comes to his senses when he exits Oníkùkùté and enters another forest called Olúbàdàn. But Akéwejè returns to Oníkùkùté the next day:

> Mo wá pe gbogbo àwọn èèyàn wa níkọ̀ọ̀kan pé kán jẹ́ ká wá lọ d'ẹgbó yẹn l'ọ̀sàn-án. A wá sígun lọ. Ẹran t'ó p'óhun ò níí fi ilẹ̀ l'óru, a wáá bá a mú mẹ́ta kúrò níbẹ̀ ní ojú gbangba.

> [I called all my people out to go and hunt that forest. So there we went that afternoon, all in arms. Out of those animals the forest was reluctant to let go in the night, we took away three in the daylight.]

The narrative of Múrítàlá Àdìgún Gbọ́dẹníyì of Tọ́lá village, Ìdó Local Government of Oyo State is set during preparation for an *ìpà*, a hunter's funeral ritual.[11] Before the ritual, the hunters always participate in a group expedition. The purpose of the expedition is not only to acquire meat for the feast, but more importantly, to procure the animal – usually the favourite kill of the deceased hunter – to be used in the rites. It is a mark of honour for a hunter to be the one to kill this animal. In Gbọ́dẹníyì's narrative, the sense of competition is heightened because the hunting party is made up of hunters from two rival communities, Tọ́lá and Sàngóòbọn. After about 12 hours of hunting without any success, Gbọ́dẹníyì suggests to his mates that they try Májàsán, a forest known to all of them as 'stingy' and difficult. They therefore demur: '*N b'ọọ mọ̀ pé Májàsán kèé fẹ́ f'ẹran rẹ̀ ẹ́ lẹ̀*' [But you know for sure Májàsán hardly lets go its animals]. Gbọ́dẹníyì then volunteers to serve as the watch for the Májàsán tunnel, the most feared area of the forest. Only then do the other hunters accede to go.

From his position, Gbọ́dẹníyì sights a deer and attempts to shoot it, but the gun fails. This failure of the gun provides the hunter a basis for the following heroic feat. He simply dispenses with the gun, whips out his machete and goes after the deer – an epic chase in the context of a tropical rain forest given the thick undergrowth and the fleet-footedness of the prey. Gbọ́dẹníyì's sighting, pursuit and catching of the deer, unaided by other hunters and dogs, is therefore rather extraordinary.

The hunter seizes the deer at the very mouth of the tunnel. With its body already halfway in, a character identified as '*ẹlẹran*' [the owner of the animal] simultaneously seizes the animal, and a struggle ensues. Like the slobbering spirit encountered by Fagunwa's Akara-ogun, the antagonist is an unidentifiable silhouette in the dark tunnel. As the struggle for the deer intensifies, the hunter invokes his father with an incantation. Even though the father does not appear materially, the hunter has enlisted him. He completes the ritual by putting in his mouth a charm bequeathed by the patriarch. And just like that, the spirit is vanquished. The hunter then dispatches the animal by slitting its throat. Thus slaughtering a deer in the same manner as a domestic animal registers the hunter's capacity to domesticate the wild. This feat, aside the coincidence of being the ritual kill, also rubs off on other Tólá hunters before their Sàngóòbọn colleagues. The protagonist is henceforth called 'Gbódẹníyì' [He-who-brings-honour-to-other-hunters].[12]

In the narrative of Yẹkíni Ọláwuyì Omítóògùn Améringùn of Ọdọ village, Ìdó Local Government of Oyo State, the hunter literally wrestles with the spirit.[13] The Heights of Jayéadé, like Fìríàáríkú's Oníwòrò, is a taboo. The hunter's decision to explore it is therefore an instance of defiance. Having hunted a nearby forest without any luck, Améringùn decides to try the forbidden mountain. The first deer he sights foreshadows the preternatural encounter he would later have: its antlers are alive with hornets and its eyes are rather too big for a deer. The hunter fires at it anyway and moves to carry the body: '*Mọ fẹẹ bẹrẹ, olówó ẹ yọ. Ibi nkán ti dé nù-un*' [But as I bent down to carry it, its owner emerged. That was where the trouble started]. Améringùn evokes the physique of the antagonist 'owner':

Àh! Èwo ni mọ ha rí yìí? Ojú u rẹ̀ báyìí, ó tó 'kúùkù . . . Irun ẹ̀, b'ó ti rí nìí gàn-ùn-gan-un. Ibi ọ́ bá gún ù'yàn báyìí, olóde ó sú n'bẹ̀ ni.

[What manner of visitation is this? Each of his eyes was as big as a human fist . . . The hair on his body was as brittle as this [indicates with an index finger]. Wherever it touched on the human body, rashes came out.]

It is with this fearful creature that the hunter struggles. '*Mo ní "Níìhín kọ́. Lónìí, aá jọ kú pọ̀ ni è"*' ['No way,' I said. 'It's going to be a fight to the finish today']. This palpable dimension of contact between the human hunter and the spirit, similar to confrontations in many of Fagunwa's stories, serves as a forceful reminder that spirits are hardly intangible entities (Gbadegesin 1998; Wiredu 1998).

In the ensuing wrestling with the spirit, the hunter's gun is of no use, as the hunter has not had time to reload it after the last shot. This handicap presents the protagonist with an opportunity to demonstrate his strength and resourcefulness. Améringùn accordingly primes his hand with a charm and breaks into incantation: '*Dàwódàwó níí s'ọmọ ewúrẹ́/Dàwódàwó níí s'ọmọ àgùntàn*' [The tender kid is never surefooted/The tender lamb is never surefooted.]

Having been dealt a slap with the hand, the spirit releases his grip and tosses about in pain, allowing the hunter some freedom to reload his gun and shoot him.

The conflict does not end, however, with the physical struggle. It continues on a more sublime but equally tense plane. Apart from the rash of smallpox that the contact sets off on the hunter's body, the spirit, now invisible, pesters the hunter at his very home. When the hunter guts and cuts up the deer, he discovers three gourdlets and four smooth pebbles in its stomach. This mystery renews the hunter's observation earlier in the narrative that upon close examination, '*Mọ wáá ri i pé ẹran yìí, osóran ni*' [I discovered it was an evil animal]. For the narrator therefore the deer and the spirit – like Akeweje's deer, rock and àràbà – are a single actant. The items found in the deer's stomach activate a hail of stones that rain each night on the roofs of the hunter and his neighbours: '*T'ọ́ bá di l'álẹ́ báyìí, gbogbo òòlé méfẹ̀ẹ̀fà tó yípoò mi, òkúta ni l'órí ẹ̀ . . . A à mọ'hun tí n fọnkúta á lù ú*' [In the nights, stones were pelted on all the six roofs surrounding my house. We did not know who it was throwing them].

There is already an implicit awareness built into the narrative that the gourdlets and the pebbles are in the same actantial class with the deer and the spirit. The hunter's insistence on keeping them for the two weeks that the stoning lasts is therefore an expression of defiance. His uncle, an elderly hunter, is educated in such matters. He instructs the hunter to surrender the items:

> *N ò ti'ẹ̀ fẹ́ kó o ó'lẹ̀; bàbá mi ní n ó kó o ó'lẹ̀ ni sẹ́. 'Sé n ọ́ b'abà jẹ́ ni?' Mo ní n ọ̀ bẹ'Lọ́un k'ábà ọ́ bàjẹ́.*

> [I initially did not want to let go the items but for my father's [uncle's] insistence. 'Do you want to throw the village into crisis?' he asked. I said I did not.]

The conflict is resolved only when the hunter is compelled by his uncle to give up the pebbles and the gourdlets, and the items are appeased by releasing them into the river. This old uncle's intervention saves the hunter's reputation as defiant, but not unreasonably so. In the gerontocentric and patriarchal social structure in which the hunter operates, the hunter's decision to give in is seen not as an inability to hold out in a fight, but rather as a noble deference to an older relation.

The stone-throwing antagonist also haunts the hunter in the narrative of Yísáù Okùnọlá Abọ̀kè of Abọ̀kè village, Lágelú Local Government, Oyo State.[14] Like Akéwejẹ̀, Abọ̀kè has lost a hare to the ìrókò tree. The hare has evidently been hit by the hunter's shot, as some parts of its intestines are seen on the ground. But the animal nevertheless flees in the direction of the ìrókò and disappears. Abọ̀kè confronts the ìrókò and warns it to release the animal or face the consequences. The next day, the hunter finds the dead hare under the tree, but as he reaches to take it, he is assailed with volleys of stones by unseen 'persons'. Bloodied, the hunter flees, leaving his bag behind. The encounter is repeated when the hunter returns to retrieve his bag. Even as the hunter triumphs in the end, this new pattern of conflict significantly challenges the stereotype of the hunter as a figure before whom all antagonists immediately give way. Only after a series of ritual invocations is the hunter able to retrieve his bag and return home without harassment. Emboldened by this success, Abọ̀kè returns once more with a magical spell and sawyers to curse the ìrókò and cut it down.

Ràfíù Ajísefínní Alájáníbọn of Ìdó village in Ìdó Local Government of Oyo State confronts the tree-spirit in human form.[15] During a group hunt, identified in the narrative as *ìlàko*, the hunters ferret out a deer and chase it towards an *ògbùngbun* tree. This particular *ògbùngbun* is established in the narrative as 'stingy', and notorious for frustrating hunters. On this very day:

> *Bí wọn se yìnbọn sí ẹran hun tó, ẹ̀yìn igbá ni wọn n yín'gbàdo ó sí. Sùngbọ́n èmi sọ fún u, mo ní: 'N'jọ́ onímí bá su'mí ẹ̀ ẹ́'lẹ̀, n'jọ́ náà ni wọn ọ kọ̀ ọ́. Tani ó su'mí ẹ̀ ẹ́'lẹ̀ tán tí ó kó o 'ápò? Kò seése. Ẹ̀yin kiní igi yìí, ẹ kọ ẹran yìí fún mi lónìí'.*

[Many as the shots fired at the animal were, none hit the target. But I spoke to *it*: '*When a man defecates, he leaves it and walks away. Does anyone defecate and put the waste in his pocket? No way. You of this tree, cede this animal to me today in the same manner.*']

From his position very close to the tree, Ajísefínní later sights the deer escaping towards it, galloping through a hail of shots with none as much as even grazing the skin. Just then, he sees an *òrò* (a tree-spirit) emerge from the tree, raising alarm: '*Ẹ̀ẹ̀ gbọdọ̀ pa mí l'ẹ́ran o*' [Never you kill my animal, I warn]. As the deer gets close to the *ògbùngbun*, Ajísefínní fires at it and hits it. The spirit immediately disappears, but a colony of ants suddenly covers the dead deer so that it becomes impossible to touch or even see it. A swarm of bees arrives as well, putting to flight all the hunters who have arrived to cut up the animal. At this point, Ajísefínní resorts to magic, '*nkan àwọn baba wa tí 'án fún wa*' [the thing bequeathed to us by our fathers], to fight back the army of ants and bees before claiming the kill.

Not all the encounters with the spirits and the animals end in straight victory for the hunter. The narrative of Múfútáù Fákáyọ̀dé Kúkúndùkú of Álúgbọ̀ Olúwo in Ẹgbẹ́dá Local Government of Oyo State illustrates a situation in which the antagonist and the protagonist match in strength.[16] During night hunting in the Forest of Afami, Kúkúndùkú is accosted by an extremely tall and brawny spirit. '*Ìwọ ọdẹ yìí*' [You hunter], the spirit calls, '*má dé inú igbó yìí mọ́. Ìkìlọ̀ ni mo fi se fún ọ o*' [never you hunt in this forest anymore from now on, I warn you].

But Kúkúndùkú, as defiant as Faguwa's Olówóayé before the spirit gatekeeper of Olodumare, retorts:

Taa n'ìwọ? . . . Gbogbo ohun t'ọọ́ bá se, èmi ọ̀ maa dé'núu'gbó yìí wáá dè'gbẹ́ o . .. Tí wọ́n bá bí ọ dáa, ijọ́ tí n bá wáá d'ẹ̀gbẹ́, wáá pàdèè mi, oó rí i pé'lẹ̀ ọ la'ná.

[Who the hell are you? . . . Do whatever you will, I shall continue to hunt in this forest . . . If you are a *man* enough, stand in my way and see the very ground under you explode as we fight.]

Soon after they part ways, the hunter sees a duiker and fires at it. The spirit hears the report of the gun, bounds towards the hunter and challenges him to a fight. As in the prolonged wrestling between Olówóayé and Ànjọ̀nú Ìbẹ̀rù (Fagunwa 1949), both the hunter and the spirit are exhausted and have to retire. As the spirit returns to his base, Kúkúndùkú takes home the duiker and instructs his wife to cook the animal's offal for his breakfast.

But early that morning, a familiar baritone wakes the hunter from his short nap, challenging him to a fight. The spirit is back in company of six other colleagues, equally tall and brawny, brandishing heavy clubs. 'Ẹtu mi dà? N'bo lọ gb'ẹtu mi sí?' [Where is my duiker? Where did you put it?], the spirit shouts and challenges the hunter to another round of fight. At the end of that fight, the hunter has been clubbed so hard that he becomes sick for about three months. The noise arising from the fight alerts the neighbours who promptly come to the hunter's house. But even as they see the hunter struggle and hear the noise of the fighting parties, the spirits are invisible to them. Elder hunters are consequently summoned; the spirits are forced to retreat under their spell.

In the hunter's logic, the current status of the Other determines the manner through which man the hunter relates to it. In the televised narrative of Tàfá Àlàdé,[17] the hunter says without any emotion: '*Bọ́ bá se p'éèyàn l'ayè, tọ́ bá tí wọnúu'gbó, tọ́ bá di ẹranko, n ọ̀ pa á*' [If even a man becomes mysterious, changes into an animal and enters the forest, I kill it]. It is a sort of acknowledgement of the impermanence through which the hunter appreciates every essence as it presents itself in the moment. In the narrative of Jọ́ọ̀gún Àlàdé (see Appendix C), the hunter sees three Fulani fetching water from his position during an expedition.[18] As they go away from the water source, a huge tree blocks each of them from the hunter's view as she passes behind it. Naturally, the three women ought to emerge and be visible again in a matter of few seconds; but three deer, not Fulani women, emerge instead. The listeners immediately deduce that the Fulani women have been transformed into animals. The hunter shoots one of the deer and goes on to carry it. He is shocked to find that one side of its body has human skin. It takes the intervention of the protagonist's father, also a hunter, to return the kill to a full status of animal whose meat would later be eaten by the community. In the narrative of Rábíù Òjó (see Appendix B), the kill is half-woman, half-civet; the hunter simply excises what is human from the meat and put the animal part on the table:

> Wón ní ẹran ọlógẹ̀dẹ̀ ni; wón ní kèé s'èèyàn. Wón ní gbogbo ẹranko t'ọ́ wà n'gbó náà ní í maá d'èèyàn á wá'lé l'álé.

> [He {an elder} said it was no more human but a civet. He said many animals in the forest often do change into human form in order to come to town anyway.]

As revolting and grim as it is to the reader, it is very simple to the hunter.

Forest the indeterminate

Despite the examples given above, the hunter's relationship to the forest should not be seen as solely one of conflict. The *fabula* that is the forest promises too much in drama to be seen solely from such a limited perspective. Admittedly, many of the hunters' narratives configure their events to favour a sort of hunter-versus-Other dichotomy, but others come in patterns that do not favour conflict. It is an under-representation of the forest's infinitude to understand the hunter-bush positionality primarily through struggle. Indeed, sometimes the hunter himself realizes the subjectivity of his position as a mythmaker who rearranges events from the jumbled past into a rather neat – and suspect because they are neat – story. He therefore begins sometimes with the reminder that that the *fabula* is too thick for his human memory, in this case in the form of the familiar proverb:

> Mélòó l'aá sọ n'núu'gbó? . . . Torí ẹni tó bá ní òwú 'ọ̀ t'ẹ́rù, 'hun tí ée tanná ló mú.

> [Can we recount all we see in the forest? No . . . It is like the cotton wool you consider light because you carry the little you need as wick].[19]

The narrative of the hunter quoted above (Àmẹ́ẹ̀dì Kókó-by-this) has three episodes. Even as there are instances of confrontation in the first two episodes, the last part, independent enough to be a narrative on its own, dispenses with such conflict. The first episode treats the hunter's encounter with an elusive deer that usually slips through the hunters' watch by barking, thereby putting the hunters under a spell. Kókó-by-this not only thwarts the deer's spell and kills the animal, but also survives the post-mortem attack that comes in the form of a headache and cold. He appropriates a gourdlet found in the animal's stomach and gives it to his father, his master and protector, for custody.

In the second episode, a week later, he traces a duiker to an *àìdan* tree where he is pitted against a spirit that wrestles with him for about ten minutes before the hunter throws him and the spirit disappears. It is at this point that palpable conflict seems to end. As Kókó-by-this hunts farther, he becomes tired and decides to rest on a particular rock where he eventually falls asleep. He wakes up later to find a covered calabash beside him. As he returns home with the item, he sees an old woman in red shorts and a white jumper – a spirit evidently – who begs him for meat so that she and her children might not starve that day. The hunter hands her a civet, his only kill for the day. The woman reciprocates the hunter's kindness by revealing to him the significance of the content of the calabash in his possession: it is used to free a woman from the visitation of *àbíkú*, a Yoruba spirit-child that torments its mother with its own repeated birth and mortality. The hunter has the calabash to this day. By neglecting the pursuit of the linear initiation of conflict and its resolution, the last third of Kókó-by-this' narrative seems to mirror with considerable fidelity the coarse *fabula* from which fine narratives are sculpted. It is this non-linear narration, with its unfettered release of events that are not necessarily organically coordinated, to which the magical realist fictions of Ben Okri and Kojo Laing aspire.

The narrative of Àpémọ̀ Kínche of Hounkoko village, Savé, Republic of Benin, opens with some promise of conflict.[20] The hunter shoots and kills a buffalo and an eland, resorting to an 'ìbora' [spell of disappearance] to make himself invisible as one of the animals rages after being wounded. Back home on the fourth day, the hunter's wife reports that two sturdy women visited and informed her that Kínche had killed a buffalo and an eland. They also left word that: '*Ẹran tí ẹ pa o, ẹran abàmì ni . . . Àwọn òwo ẹran yìí, gbogbo ẹ̀ n kẹẹ kó sí'dìì Ògún o. K'ẹẹ rì í mọ́'lẹ̀ n'bẹ́ k'ẹẹ máa bọ ọ́ o'* [The animals you have killed are strange ones . . . Put their horns in the shrine of Ogun. Bury them there and offer sacrifice to them].

The hunter later seeks clarification from his *babaláwo* who reveals that the visitors are the very animals the hunter had killed. If he adheres to their instruction, says the *babaláwo*, he will be lucky in his future expeditions. Kínche tries the ritual and finds it true:

> *Lóòtọ̀, bẹ́ẹ̀ sì ní n rí. Tí n bá ti súre n'bẹ̀ látàárọ̀ tàbí l'álẹ́, tí n ba ti gbé'bọn, ẹran ó kú.*
>
> [Truly things happen accordingly. Whenever I offer the prayers there {at the shrine}, be it in the morning or night, and take out my gun, an animal certainly will die.]

A conundrum emerges – why is this animal, whom the hunter has shot and killed, suddenly offering to become the hunter's ally? The hunter does not claim to totally comprehend the 'strange ways of the forest'. He only sees, survives, marvels and continues with his expedition.

Like other hunters discussed here, the narrative of Olúsẹ́gun Àkànjí Kúlakùla of Aràrọ̀mí village, Aperin, Ìbàdàn, Oyo State, also includes the killing of an elusive deer that belongs to a rock-spirit.[21] Kúlakùla's narrative, however, has none of the wrestling, shooting and casting of spells that usually characterise the hunter-spirit face-off. The hunter simply goes home with the kill and has a good lunch of its offal. Three days later however, he is accosted by an old man in rags who identifies the hunter by his name. The old man tells him:

> Ìgalà t'ọ́ọ pa n'jẹta, ẹran àwọn àgbàlagbà ni o. Sì rí i p'óo s'ètùtù rẹ̀ daadáa. K'ọ́ọ wá obì funfun olójú mẹ́'ndínlógún, obì pupa olójú mẹ́'ndínlógún.

> [The deer you killed three days ago belonged to the powerful ones. Make sure you carry out its ritual appeasement properly. You must look for a white cola nut of sixteen lobes and red one of sixteen lobes.]

The old man might be seen in the mode of Helper described by French aesthetician Etienne Souriau, come to warn the hunter-hero before the spirit-deer opponent arrives in vengeance. But that equilibrium is unsettled by the fact that the deer, the supposed opponent, doubles as the helper. According to Kúlakùla's *babaláwo*, 'ìgalà t'ọ́ọ pa n lọ́ wáá pàdé è rẹ. Àwọn ètùtù yìí, lóòtọ́ l'oó se é' [it was the very deer you killed that came to you {in human form}. You must carry out the prescribed ritual accordingly]. Here therefore is a rare situation in which the potential antagonist tells the hunter how to contain it.

The hunter himself is sometimes merely a witness to the forest's prismatic weirdness, playing not more than the role of cinema audience. In another narrative of Jọ́ọgún Áládè of Ọ̀jẹ́ Owódé, Oyo State, the hunter is a mere youth not old enough to use the gun.[22] In company of his father during a night hunt, the young hunter keeps watch over a tunnel under the light of the full moon. Just then, drumming and music rend the air; a choir of porcupines files out of the tunnel all dressed in 'ẹ̀wù ẹtù' [ceremonial attires made from a traditional Yoruba textile], singing and dancing to *dùndún* [talking drums] and *sẹ̀kẹ̀rè* [rattlers made of gourd and cowries]. Little Jọ́ọgún watches in fear from his position, while the older hunter does not shoot at the animals. The father will later tell Jóòògún and his brothers that he would have shot at the animals if he had wanted to, but he feared that they (the children) might want to do the same in future, an action that might prove fatal for them as they are too young to know how to ward off the ensuing danger. From that day, the father forbids them to watch the tunnels, whether in his company or alone. Meanwhile, he begins an elaborate process of fortifying his sons with supernatural powers.

Akínwándé Akíntáyọ̀ of Àjóyìnbọn village similarly sees giant rats in concert. Hunting in the Forest of Ilẹ̀ Pupa, the hunter sights the rodents from a high vantage, dancing on their hind legs round an anthill. Apparently made shy by a bitter experience (cited in the next chapter) in which a curse was placed on him, the hunter refrains from shooting and diverts himself by simply watching the rodents perform.[23]

Man the hunter is not situated in eternal opposition to the wild. The forest is not a simple landscape only waiting in order that the hunter might colonise it. The forest is instead a realm of uncertainty that the hunter explores in order that mankind may have knowledge. As will be shown in the next chapter, it is in the context of that uncertainty that the forest, many times, subdues the hunter.

Notes

1. *Ceiba Pentandra.*

2. *Ọdẹ Akọni*, 24/12/2006.

3. For example, ọ̀rọ̀-hùnùhùnù in Òfún Méjì (Abimbola 1969:100–105).

4. *Chlorophora excelsa.*

5. *Ọdẹ Akọni*, 01/08/2004.

6. Personal interaction, 26/0220/06.

7. Personal interaction, 22/04/2006.

8. *Ọdẹ́tẹ̀dó*, n.d.

9. *Ọdẹ Akọni*, 13/06/2004.

10. *Ceiba pentandra.*

11. *Ọdẹ Akọni*, 03/06/2007.

12. *Ọdẹ Akọni*, 03/06/2007.

13. *Ọdẹ Akọni*, 12/09/2004.

14. *Ọdẹ Akọni*, 19/09/2004.

15. Personal interaction, 25/09/2005.

16.   *Ọdẹ Akọni*, 29/07/2007.

17.   *Ọdẹtẹdo* n.d.

18.   Personal interaction, 16/12/2006.

19.   Tàòfíkì Àmẹ̀ẹ̀dì Kókó-by-this, Akínẹ̀rín village, Ìwó Osun State. Personal interaction, 20/11/2005.

20.   Personal interaction, 02/05/2006. Kínche currently lives in Ìgbínjẹ village, Ilé Ogbó, Ọsun State.

21.   *Ọdẹ Akọni*, 18/11/2007.

22.   Personal interaction, 16/12/2006.

23.   *Ọdẹ Akọni*, 08/05/2005.

4

Negotiating the Formidable

Introduction

His occasional declamation notwithstanding, the hunter's position is precarious. He explores the realm of the uncertain, and implicitly stands imperilled, for he cannot totally pacify the forest antagonist who is not entirely known to him. This predicament is complicated by the realisation that the forest occasionally merges with home, thereby making the hunter's antagonist engagement with it more difficult.

The hunter, the Other and the limits of man

The hunter sometimes imagines himself to be a superior partner in the cosmos he shares with the rest of creation. I interpret this imagination and its narrative expression as part of the hunter's commitment to confronting the formidable. The hero of the narrative of Ògúnwálé Ọlaníyì Bíòkú most certainly sees himself in this light. Protected by Ikúlòògùn, his master, and having transgressed two physical borders without coming to any harm, he is emboldened to declare in the face of an antagonistic spirit:

> *Gbogbo ohun tí ń mí àt'èyí tí èé mí tí Ọlọun dá l'Ọlọun jù lọ. Ọlọun sì ti fi àwa, ó ti fi wá se olórí . . . Ọgbọn hóró kan ló sì wà nínú u tiyín. Kò s'ọnà t'áwa ò lè ya ọgbọn sí láti r'éyìn yín. T'èmi j'agbára tiè lọ.*

> [God is greater than everything he created – both the ones that breathe and the ones that don't. And God has made us [mankind] lord over all . . . You {non-human beings} have only one wit but man has a lot of ways through which he could tame you. I was stronger than he was therefore.][1]

Yet, as I noted earlier, in many ways, the Yoruba worldview does not privilege man's superordinate status in relation to all other earthly creation. The idea that man is the centre of earthly creation (Mbiti 1975) is a formulation thrown up by the received cultures of Europe and Arabia. Soyinka, dramatist, poet and social interventionist, exploits this Yoruba anti-anthropocentric consciousness as part of his recurrent thematic premise that man is vulnerable, sinful and in continuous need of redemption. In Soyinka's *A Dance of the Forest* (1963), which is an examination of the underside of human history in a decade when African nations rapidly gained political independence and the resulting hysteria inhibited introspection, he prescribes that man must develop humility and self-appraisal as he enters the politically independent half of his history. These qualities are non-negotiable if man is to achieve redemption. In the play, deities and spirits collaborate to expose the hubris of man, both living and ancestral. It is from the acknowledgement and proof of man's weakness and inadequacy that the quest for salvation draws its *raison d'être*.

Fagunwa's largely anthropocentric Christian vision notwithstanding, his treatment of man the hunter considerably limits man's claims to superiority. Encountering Èsù-kékeré-òde, the one-eyed elf for the first time, Olówóayé, the hunter-protagonist of *Igbó Olódùmarè*, retorts to the spirit's challenge:

> Ẹni ti o fi aṣẹ gbe ojo o tan ara rẹ̀ jẹ; ẹni ti o duro de reluwe, yio ba ara rẹ̀ ni ọrun alakeji; agba ti o ri ejo ti ko sa ara iku l'o nya a; ẹranko ti o ba fi oju di ọdẹ ẹhin ãro ni yio sun: ẹniti o gboju le ogun fi ara rẹ̀ fun oṣi ta; ẹbọra ti o ba f'oju di mi yio ma ti ọrun de ọrun ni, emi ọkunrin ni mo wi bẹ, oni ni ng o sọ fun ẹyin ẹbọra Igbó Olódùmarè pe, nigbati Ẹlẹda da ohun gbogbo ti mbẹ ninu aiye tan, o fi enia ṣe olori gbogbo wọn.

> [Whoever fetches water with a sieve deceives himself; anyone who stands in the way of a moving train is courting death; a man who sees a poisonous snake and does not flee is tired of living; the animal that defies the hunter will end up cooked; a lazy man that relies on inherited wealth has handed himself up to poverty; any spirit that dares me will die many times over, I, a strong man, assure you. *Today, I shall prove to you all the spirits of the Forest of Olódùmarè that after God created all the things on earth, he made man their lord* [my italics] (Fagunwa 1949:16).]

The subsequent wrestling between the spirit and the hunter does not favour the hunter's boast. In that struggle, the hunter realises that he does not stand any chances against the impregnable elf. He therefore resorts to diplomacy through poetry sung '*tanutanu* [pitifully]' (Fagunwa 1949:19). Only then is Èsù-kékeré-òde appeased and the hunter allowed to go. It is possible that Fagunwa meant to insist on man's rational superiority to spirits, given Olówóayé's sagacious resort to diplomacy when brawn fails him. Olówóayé and Fagunwa's other hunter-protagonists, however, arguably only survive through their immunity as heroes; this is the conventional immunity they require as fictional constructs to live until the end of their stories. Lesser hunter-characters are not so lucky. In *Ogbójú ọdẹ nínú Igbó Irúnmalẹ̀* (Fagunwa 1950b:44–45), Lamọrin, a hunter and friend of the protagonist, is devoured by Tèmbèlèkun, a cannibal spirit, without being able to put up a fight, while the protagonist himself, through stealth, barely escapes with his life.

In the Yoruba hunters' narratives, man is constantly reminded of the precarious impermanence of his position in the dialogic community where participants contest, sometimes mortally, for primacy. It is therefore part of the hunter's calling to design and deploy strategies not only to subdue the Other, but also sometimes to recognise the Other's equal, or even superior, status. The narrative of Kìlání Alápó of Alápó village, Ibadan, Oyo State, foregrounds the awareness that the powerful Other must be tamed through negotiation, not confrontation.[2] Early in the narrative, it is established that the hunter has, once for each of the past eight years, killed a python under a particular àràbà tree in the Forest of Elérè. In the ninth year of Alápó's annual 'harvest' of python, the hunter does not see a python under the àràbà, as usual, but instead finds an 'awo ìgalà' [deer's skin]. The preternatural aspect of the skin is that it comes whole as if the life and flesh in it had simply liquefied and seeped out through its eyeholes, leaving the skin intact: no cut, no seam. The narrator quickly modifies the name of the item in view of this, saying, 'Tàbí kí nsó wípé àwo ò 'galà n l'odè bá n'bè – àwo ò 'galà t'ígalà bóó 'lè torítesè' [Or better put, the hunter saw a slough cast off by a deer]. An Àwo [slough] therefore equates the item to the layer of skin naturally cast off by snakes, highlighting the weirdness, as living bovines do not shed their skins in such a manner.

Various Yoruba narratives feature animals similarly shedding their skins in order to transform into man. Two hunter stories in *Dahomean Narrative: A Cross-cultural Analysis* (Herskovits and Herskovits 1958) relate the hunter's confiscation of such a slough [àwo] and the subsequent marriage between the hunter and the animal, who turned into a beautiful woman. In one version of the story of the wedlock of Oya (a Yoruba deity) and Ògún, set down by Adepegba (2008), Ògún the primordial hunter and deity of hunting likewise confiscates Oya's àbíkú costume of buffalo hide and horns. She is therefore bonded in marriage to the hunter in whose custody she 'keeps' her real form and her secret. In all these narratives and others like them, the hunter-animal liaison ends in woe for the hunter. Even when the hunter comes out alive, he often loses his wife and children in the emergent struggle with the vindictive animal who is bent on annihilating the hunter's family to avenge his sin of indiscretion and/or insult.

As Alápó goes home with the àwo, he therefore does so with the full understanding of the capacity of a 'human' out of animal's skin to visit misery on the hunter. It is in his resolution to take home the àwo that his bravery is inscribed. His apprehension of the possible adverse consequences of keeping the àwo later makes him so uneasy that he resorts to consulting the *babálawo*. He is warned by the diviner to keep it safe, for '*aláwọ̀ ọ́ wàá bééré áwọ́*' [the owner is coming back for her slough].

On the seventh day after his return, a beautiful fair-complexioned woman arrives at Alápó village and asks to be shown to Kìlání Alápó's house. Her arrival is greeted by the frantic baying and barking of dogs who '*pa kuuru ú mọ́ ọ*' [charged at her as if they would attack]. The character of the dog, itself a hunter, is an ancillary representation of the hunter's far-sightedness. As animals with a capacity for sensing the numinous, the dogs' frenzy creates foreshadowing. In camera with the hunter, the woman goes immediately to the subject of her visit: '*Ẹ dákun, àwọ̀ mi t'ẹ́ẹ kó, mọ fẹ́ k'ẹ́ẹ kó o fún mi*' [Would you please return my slough?]. The hunter agrees to return it at an appointed time and place. He schedules another meeting with the woman under the àràbà in the night. In order to ensure confidentiality and to prevent interruption by a third party, the hunter sets out for the appointed place rigged out as if on his regular hunting routine. He finds the woman waiting and hands over her àwọ̀. The deer-woman rewards Kìlání Alápó for his faithfulness by promising him a deer each year. For the past 15 years, the hunter has killed a deer every year under the tree.

Whereas Alápó is rewarded for knowing his place and limitation as *man*, Nathaniel Ògúnlékè Ògúnọ̀sun gets the hard knocks.[3] In the narrative of Ògúnkúnlé Òjó of Agúnrege, Oyo State, Ògúnọ̀sun, the narrator's master, marries a buffalo (see Appendix D). The narrative adjusts very early to the hunter's magical reality as Ògúnkúnlé, the hunter's understudy, travels a distance of 45 miles on foot in just under three minutes to report to his master at home that he had felled a buffalo. As they both return to the forest, about a mile from the spot, '*àfi pẹ̀kí n la bá pàdé ẹran lọ́nà, èyuùn ìyàwó. Arẹwa obinrin ni*' [we ran into the animal, that is, the wife. She was a very beautiful woman]. The narrator's compounding of the animal and the woman implies that the felled animal has transformed into a human. Like Olówóayé, enchanted by the *àjẹ́* woman the former runs into in the Forest of Olódùmarè, Ògúnọ̀sun makes advances to the woman.

It is the same principle of domestication that underlies the hunter's insistence that nothing is wrong in putting an animal killed in the most strange and weird circumstances on the table that also normalises liaisons between men and animals-turned-women. A deer that had, ten minutes before, been an old woman, makes good meat, in the same way that a beautiful woman – who used to be a rhesus monkey – makes a fine second wife. Non-hunters may find this revolting, but it is nevertheless one of the bases upon which the hunter is considered the communal limen between the Same and the wild preternatural Other.

Ògúnọ̀sun woos the woman, asking for her hand in marriage. She agrees, with an already familiar condition:

Nlọ p'ọ́ọ́ fẹ́ òhun yìí o. T'íjà bá dé o, n'jọ́ t'ọ́ọ bá p'òhun l'ọmọ ẹranko, n'jọ́ náà ni títán dé bá ọ ò. Ò báà nà'hun, k'ọ́ọ sá'hun l'ọ́gbẹ́ k'ẹ́jẹ̀ ọ́ máa jáde l'ára òhun, kò s'íhun tí ọ́ ṣẹlẹ̀.

[Now that you insist on marrying me, be informed that the day you, out of anger, call me an animal, that day would be your last. It would not offend me as much if you hit me so much that I am wounded and bleeding.]

This prohibition sets the stage for the subsequent conflict. The buffalo-woman remains the hunter's wife long enough to bear him three children. Then, one day, a quarrel ensues, and the hunter explodes: '*Àb'órí ì rẹ burú ni, ìwọ ọmọ ẹranko yìí*' [You good-for-nothing unlucky daughter of an animal] and '*ibi wàhálà ti dé nùun*' [that was where the trouble started]. The woman is at once seized by a paroxysm of anger in which she is transformed into a buffalo, bristling with vengeance. The hunter, now helpless and a fugitive, runs towards Ìgbàdì, a prehistoric mountain on the outskirts of the village, where the buffalo catches up with him. The buffalo gores him badly before fleeing into the forest, never to return. The hunter survives the attack, but limps from the resulting fracture in his leg until his death.

Ásìmíyù Ògúndépò Pabíẹkùn of Ìdí Ògún village, Ságbẹ́, Ibadan, Oyo State, wrestles with a female spirit in a broadcast narrative (see Plate 4.1).[4] As in Ògúnkúnlé's narrative, the classification of the antagonist as female, well outlined in a skirt, is meant to attenuate the hunter's status as a man whose machismo ordinarily subordinates the woman. The narrative is set in the night, beginning with the hunter's initial failure to locate any game in a particular unnamed forest. He then decides to go to the Forest of Olókè where '*Igi ahùn kan n bẹ n'bẹ̀, àbáláyé ahùn ni; rábátá bàyíí l'ahùn náà. Àwa bá a l'áyé ni. Àwọn t'ó jù wá lọ gaan bá a l'áyé ni*' [There was an *ahùn* tree, so ancient that it was older than even our own elders, and very big too].

Plate 4.1: Pabíẹkùn (right) performing his narrative while Báyọ̀ Adébọ̀wálé (background) interjects with flute and Kọ́lá Akíntáyọ̀ (left) listens

Pabíẹkùn sights a duiker under the tree and shoots it. As he moves in to retrieve the animal, '*ìyá hun bá b'óóde t'òhun ti tòbí n'dìí*' [a woman in skirt emerged]. Even as the narrative does not exclusively categorise the 'woman' as a spirit, her occurrence at that place and time immediately qualifies her as one. Subsequent events in the narrative establish this more convincingly. The woman accuses the hunter of wanting to steal her animal, and stands in his way as if to prevent him from leaving with the game. The resulting struggle lasts for a couple of hours with neither of the two parties gaining the upper hand. At some point, the hunter fumbles for his machete and makes to cut the animal in two, so that he may take the upper part, leaving the hindquarters for the spirit. Pabíękùn's resolution is an admission of his inability to subdue the woman. But the spirit, rather than having the hunter split the animal in two, makes an appeal in which she discloses that her husband is the owner of the duiker, and

> ọkọ ọ'hun, òhun u rè 'ọ jọọ gbé'núu 'gbó yìí. Ọtọ̀ n'ibi t'ọkọ ọ'hun ngbé. Ó sì ti rìn'rìn àjò. T'ọ́ bá sì e dé tí ọ̀ bá e bá ẹran yìí tàbí t'óhun ọ̀ bá r'ókù u rè̩ gbé fún u pé nkankan lọ́ p'ẹran yìí…inú ọkọ ọ̀'hùn le é'pọ̀ o. Lílé ní ó lé 'hun b'óóde o.

[her husband lived separately in a different forest. He had, in fact, gone on a journey. If he returned, she continued, and found the animal missing, and she could not show him the body to prove the animal had been killed, that would be the end of their marriage. Her husband was so mean. He would simply throw her out.]

And the spirit makes an offer:

> Ó ní'hun t'óhun lè se fún mi t'ée pé t'ọ́jọ́ ọ'kú ee dé, òhun ó fún mi tí ọ́ j'ánfààní. Nítorí i p'étu yìí, t'óhun bá yọ̀nda è̩ fún mi, pátápátá, ijọ́ márùn-ún, ijọ́ méfà, kí n fi jẹ é̩ àt'èmi àt'àwọn ará íléè mi. Sùgbọ́n oore àjẹè̩jẹtán l'òhun ó fún mi.

[She then said that there was a favour she could do me that I would profit from till death; for this duiker would surely not last me more than five days or six as food, for me and my household. But what she would give me in its place would be of eternal benefit.]

The spirit then fetches a gourdlet from inside her skirt and offers it to the hunter. According to her, the gourdlet contains a charm for hypnotising animals. She describes its application:

> Gbogbo ibikíbi t'ọ́ọ bá ti dé lọ́sàn-án, tí èé s'òru o, t'ọ́ọ bá ti r'ójú ẹsẹ̀ ẹran, irú ẹranko t'ọ́ yẹ ọ́ jẹ́ l'áyé, t'ọ́ọ bá e sí àdó yìí, t'ọ́ ọ gbọ̀n ọ́ s'ójú ẹsẹ̀ ẹ rẹ̀, lọ wá'bìkan jókòó sí. Ìgbà tí ọ bá e tó ìdátọ̀mì márùn-ún, ẹran hun ó rín wá bá ọ. Ọ ó kàn pa à n'ípakúpa ni.

[Whenever you are hunting in the daylight – not in the night, please – any footprints of an animal you see, put some of the contents of the gourdlet on it and find a place to mount watch. Before long, the animal would come to you. You would kill it as easily as that.]

Having handed the hunter the gourdlet, she vanishes with the duiker, leaving the hunter in a momentary daze and a cold shiver. The next day, Pabíękùn tries the charm and accordingly kills a duiker and an antelope. In *Ogbójú ọdẹ*, Akara-ogun, the protagonist, mischievously wangles a similar charm from *Árọ̀ní*, the monopedal spirit.

Moses Ògúnwálé of Ifẹ̀ Ọ̀dàn, Èjìgbò Local Government, Osun State, tells a story in which he emerges with a similar souvenir, but more humbled.[5] He admits that '*wọ́n le jù mí lọ*' [they {the spirits} are tougher than I am] (see Plate 4.2).

Plate 4.2: Ògúnwálé (right) performing while Akíntáyọ̀ (left) listens

Hunting the Heights of Ọbaálá on a Sunday night, a pair of deer's eyes reflects in the hunter's light. The hunter shoots at the animal, only to see those reflecting eyes multiply into 14, that is, seven deer. He then trains his light more intently on the animals and fires in the middle, at the smallest of the herd. As it falls, the rest of the eyes disappear. When Ògúnwálé goes to inspect the animal, he is accosted by hands whose owners are identified as '*awọn irunmọlẹ*' or '*awọn iwin inu u'gbo*' [the spirits of the forest] with whom the hunter is forever engaged in conflict. In a struggle that lasts until the early hours of the next morning, the spirits not only attempt to deny the hunter the kill but, more importantly, also apprehend him as the police do a petty thief. The hunter is eventually dragged into a vast subterranean settlement, the village of the spirits:

> *Nínúu kòtò hun, mọ b'áwọn èèyàn n'bẹ̀. Àwọn èèyàn hun 'ọ̀ wá ga tó wa. Sùgbọ́n wọ́n sanra . . . Ilé nbẹ, gbogbo ẹ̀ nbẹ . . . Ilé hun rí pẹkutupẹkutu bí ilée Fílàní báyìí.*

> [In this underground place, I met *people* there. But they were not as tall as we {humans} are. But they were fat . . . There were houses and all . . . The houses were as squat as the Fulani huts.]

The underground, like trees and rocks, is also home to spirits. Lindfors (1973) writes that in the narratives of Amos Tutuola, the underground is one of the major settings portrayed as home to the spirit characters. Human characters who fall or stray into the underground are pitted as intruders against the spirit residents (Lindfors 1973:62). Countless other examples abound in Fagunwa's work, one very memorable example being the multitude of elves summoned from the underground by Ògòngò, the avian monarch.

Ògúnwálé is detained underground for seven days, surviving on such emergency hunters' provisions as roasted corn and plantain. Even in detention, the hunter still considers himself a man of strength, for as the spirits inspect him from afar, as men do a notorious burglar on parade, none is able to venture near because '*ọgbọ́n àwọn àgbà tí n bẹ l'ára ọ̀ jẹ́ wọn ó le súnmọ́ mi*' [the ancient magical power I had been fortified with did not allow them to come near]. Perhaps out of pity for the hunter's condition – for he has declined to eat the unidentifiable meal served him by the spirits – his captors release him on the seventh day with a stern warning never to come near their livestock again. Though the hunter continues to defy the spirits in his retort that God, not the spirits, is the owner of animals, he is at that point a beaten man. Before he is magically transported above ground, the hunter is given two gourdlets: the first contains a medicine that heals haemorrhoids and the second a medicine for healing ulcers. Once more, the inexplicable leniency and benefaction challenge our normative expectation in the relation between antagonists.

For the Yoruba hunter, alternative life and consciousness are not found only in terrestrial spaces like trees, rivers, rocks and underground. The aerial world also shares a boundary with man and participates in the dialectic of confrontation and negotiation. In the narrative of Kọ̀bọmọjẹ́ Àlàdé of Látúndé village, Ìdí Ayùnré, Ibadan, Oyo State, the protagonist strays into one such aerial territory, survives and returns home grateful for his life (see Appendix F).[6] The Heights of Ẹbẹdí in Ìséyìn (Òkè-Ògùn area of Oyo State) creeps with prime game, but hunting there at night is forbidden. Kọ̀bọmọjẹ́, a hunter settler from Ibadan, has been informed by his Ìséyìn colleagues that certain malignant spirits would thwart any hunter that trespasses Ẹbẹdí at night, sometimes fatally. Kọ̀bọmọjẹ́ nevertheless steals to the mountain one night. After hunting for many hours without success, he sees a pair of eyes reflecting his light. As he aims and makes to shoot, he hears the sound of bells in the air far above, getting louder as it rapidly approaches.

Like any other Yoruba hunter, Kọ̀bọmọjẹ́ knows that *àjà*, the spirit of the wind, is manifest in jingles and whirlwinds: '*a à ti mọ̀ p'áàjà ló ni sawòro?*' [who does not know that *àjà* comes in jingles?]. He has also heard narratives about humans abducted by *àjà*, fed only seven seeds of alligator pepper daily during the seven years of their incarceration. Kọ̀bọmọjẹ́ does not want any of that, so he flees. But even in flight, the hunter still considers his nocturnal foray and safe return a feat of bravery. He credits it to the magical protection bequeathed to him:

> *Ọlá àwọn tí'án fi mí l'ọ́kàn balẹ̀ pé kò s'íbi tí mo lè lọ, kò níí s'éwu, wọ́n gbé lú'a ẹ̀ lọ nù un.*

[If not for the assurance I had been given that wherever I went, no evil would befall me, I would have ended up taken away by the wind.]

Even then, he is not under any illusion that he stands any chance before the whirlwind. He promptly renounces going to Ẹbẹdí, even in the daylight:

N 'ò dé'bẹ̀ mọ́ o. N 'ọ̀ gbọdọ̀ p'arọ́ n'íwájú Ògún o . . . Tọr 'ẹ́ni ààjà bá gbé lọ, bí ọ̀ bá pẹ́ẹ́'pọ̀ ní ọ́ l'ọdún méje . . . Ataare nìkan náà ní ọ maa jẹ f'ódidi ọdún méje hun.

[Let me not lie to you, for Ogun sees me; I stopped going to hunt in that place . . . Whoever is taken by *ààjà*, mind you, is kept away for at least seven years . . . And such person would be fed on a sole diet of alligator pepper those seven years.]

The admission that the hunter is sometimes powerless before the Other is demonstrated in the ritual sacrifice he sometimes offers before entering a notorious forest. In the narrative of Músá Ìbàrìbá of Àgọ́-Àrẹ́, Oyo State, the hunter appeases the spirits of the Forest of Aláàáyá in this way.[7] But even then, every animal he shoots vanishes as soon as the bullet hits it. Having hunted for six days without luck, he dreams on the seventh day that he is being led by his *babaláwo* into the forest, but a particular truculent spirit refuses them entry, insisting, despite the old priest's entreaties, that they go back or face untoward consequences. Ìbàrìbá reads the dream as a warning from a stronger foe. He promptly returns home.

The Forest of Yaríyarí, hunted by Omíjàyí Àtàndá, the Olúọ́dẹ of Ajagunlaàsẹ̀ town, Osun State, is equally intimidating:[8] 'Igbó yìí, igbó abàmì gbáá ni. T'ọdẹ ọ́ bá d'ẹgbó yìí, ọdẹ gbọdọ̀ s'ètùtù' [The forest is very strange and weird indeed. The hunter has to offer a sacrifice before hunting in it].[9] Like Ìbàrìbá, Omíjàyí offers the sacrifice before beginning the day's hunting but fails nevertheless to kill any animals. Returning home at about two o'clock in the afternoon, the hunter stops over at a stream in the forest to have a quick bath. There, he meets two other men he thinks are hunters. After the bath, he shares their pomade before setting out for home. But as the hunter gets closer to home, none of the people he meets greet him or respond to his greeting. Once at home, the hunter meets with no enthusiastic relations, as is customary; no one welcomes him. So, Omíjàyí goes to his bedroom angry, wondering why his late return should be such an enormous offence. Irked by his rude reception, the hunter, after some rest and a change of clothes, visits his elder brother in the adjoining compound to report his offending family members. But once again, no one, including his brother, recognizes his presence with as much as a stare. Leaving angry, he heads for the house of his best friend. There he is equally ignored.

In the meantime, members of the Omíjàyí family have started to fuss about the failure of the hunter to return from the forest. Meeting them in the midst of their deliberations on how to deploy men to look for him on his farm and in the forest, Omíjàyí, still sulking, tells them: '*Sé èmi lè nwáá lọ? Èmi rèé o. Ẹnìkankan ọ́ má wá èmi lọọ'bìkankan o*' [What is this nonsense about looking for me? I am right here. Let no one waste his time looking for me]. No one responds. At this point, it dawns on the hunter that his material presence is no longer felt. For three days, he follows the different search parties dispatched to look for him, distraught and miserable, shouting himself hoarse, '*Èmi rèé, kínní n se yín gan-àn? Ẹ 'íì màá s'èèyàn daada à. Mo l'émi rèé. Sé gbogbo yín pawópọ̀ nítorìí mi ni?*' [Here I am. Is anything the matter with you? See me here. Have all of you conspired against me?]. Frustrated in his bid to be heard and seen, the hunter returns to the Yaríyarí Forest, and, after two days of wandering, retires to the river bank. The two men from whom Omíjàyí took the pomade five days ago come by again, greet him and acknowledge his response. Relieved to find the first human companionship in five days, Omíjàyí plunges into a torrent of complaints about his present condition. The men, themselves surprised, quiz him:

'*Sé ìwọ t'ọ́ọ gbà'para, séèé s'araa wa ni?*'
'*Ara a yín b'óo?*'
'*Àwa èé s'èèyàn bíi t'iyín.*'
'*Èhn! Ẹ 'íì s'èèyàn? Ẹdú'ó, sé ìpara tí mo fi para ni ọ̀ jẹ́ wọn ó rí mi n'lé?*'
'*Eèé s'ará ayé mọ́.*'

['Were you not one of us before you took the pomade?'
'One of you?'
'Yes, for we are not human as you are'
'You are not human? Wait a minute; is it the pomade that I used that has made me invisible at home?'
'Yes, you are no more of the human world.']

With the issue thus clarified, Omíjàyí prays profusely for the 'men' to return him to his original state. Moved, the two 'men' collect some herbs and instruct the hunter to take a bath, sponging himself with the herbs. After the bath, Omíjàyí returns home to a jubilant welcome from family and friends, now frustrated in their futile search. He could only convince them he had been home before by his clothing, which was not his regular hunting gear.

Hunters frequently poach in forbidden territory, often in full awareness that they are doing so. When confronted with the accusation of 'stealing' from this 'Othered' territory, they deflect the responsibility to Ògún, their patron deity. Tafa Alade, one of the hunters cited in Chapter 3, says:

*Hun t'Ògún-ún bá ti yàn fún mi, n ọ́ pa á. Bí n bá ǹ lọ nínú u'gbó o tèmi jẹ́ẹ́jẹ́,
bí n bá pàdé erin, erin ti d'òkú nùun, ǹkan ọbẹ̀ baba à mi ni, Ògún ti pa á . .
. Ògún lọ́ l'ẹran. Bọ́ bá se p'éèyàn l'ayè, tọ́ bá tí wọnúu'gbó, tọ́ bá di ẹranko,
n ọ́ pa á.*

[Whatever Ògún has elected to give me is what I kill. When I walk the forest
alone and I meet the elephant, the elephant falls dead; elephant is meat to my
forefathers; Ògún kills it . . . Ògún owns the animal. If even a man becomes
mysterious, changes into an animal and enters the forest, I kill it].[10]

Also, when the brawny spirit, accompanied by his six mates, takes the battle to the
homestead of Fákáyọ̀dé Kúkúndúkù and asks the hunter to produce the duiker he
'stole', the hunter quickly reminds him that the animal belongs to the deity, and
that it was the deity that shot and killed it. Invoking the deity is one device that the
hunter regularly employs to fend off collision with the vengeful Other. Sometimes,
however, the antagonist Other disregards the hunter and his god. The *àjẹ́* is one
such character. Layiwola (1987) reveals that Olódùmarè, the Yoruba Supreme
Being, has ceded to the *àjẹ́* a measure of energy to allow them a place in the same
supernatural corridor with the deities, even while denying them actual divinity. It is
therefore not necessarily profane when the woman agent of the *àjẹ́* disregards the
hunter's Ògún immunity, since she somewhat belongs in the same plane with the
god. The hunter character in the narrative of Ọláníyì Ọládèjọ Yáwọ́ọrẹ́ of Òbọdà
village, Ẹgbẹ́dá Local Government, Oyo State, knows this, and his management of
the conflict with an *àjẹ́* character illustrates the hunter's acknowledgement of the
àjẹ́ as a formidable force.[11]

Yáwọ́ọrẹ́ is on the trail of a notorious deer that has for many years eluded other
hunters (see Appendix E). Finally, sighting it breastfeeding its kid, the hunter aims
the gun at it. But at the moment that he makes to fire, he is struck by a dizziness that
blurs his vision. By the time he applies charms and incantation to fight the 'attack',
the deer has already been alerted and is in flight. The hunter nevertheless gives it
chase, finally felling it. Having cut the tips of the animal's ears and tail as proof that
he killed it, as is the custom, the hunter leaves to invite his mates to help with the
gutting and cutting up. On their arrival, they find the animal on its feet, bristling and
ready to gore anyone that comes near.[12] The animal's cut ears are enough evidence
to the other hunters that the deer has gone through one 'death', so none of them
wants to shoot it the second time. On the order of Yáwọ́ọrẹ́, an attempt is made to
shoot the animal again, but the gun simply fails to fire. The hunter then whips out
an *igbàdí*, a charm belt, from around his waist and flogs the animal with it, killing
it (again) instantly.

After flaying the deer and cutting up the flesh, the hunter spreads out the skin in the open at home to dry. This is the point where the *àjé* comes in. Liaisons between *àjé* and the hunter – or the *àjé* and any other person for that matter – are possible, usually resulting in the hunter's success and protection against all contrary forces. In turn, the hunter is expected to be humble and respectful not only to women, any of whom could be an *àjé*, but to everyone. One term of this contract is that the human beneficiary should not be extravagant in the display of his success. While for certain hunters, the *àjé* represents a devil not worth dining with, even with a long spoon, some believe the *àjé* energy could be managed positively to the hunter's advantage. Julius Okelola of Saki, for example, holds that the *àjé* is a finicky ally who would certainly turn into an animal and devour the hunter in the end, for when the hunter dissatisfies her, '*lílọ t'ọ́ bée lọ, t'ọ́dẹ nì ọ bá múra, wọn ó gbókùú ẹ wá'lé ni*' [the next expedition he embarks upon would be his last if that hunter is not well fortified].[13]

Radio host, Kọ́lá Akíntáyọ̀, a hunter and presenter of *Ọdẹ Akọni*, reflects differently on this *àjé* complex:

> *B'èèyàn bá l'óhun ò níí júbà àwọn tó l'ayé kó tó maa jẹ'nje ayé, irú wọn a kú n'ígbà tí'ọ̀ tọ́'jọ́ . . . B'ó tí waa wú kì wọn wà lẹ́yìn èèyàn tó, èèyàn gbọ́dọ̀ níwàà'rẹ̀lẹ̀, torí oníwàà'rẹ̀lẹ̀ l'àwọn ìyá hun.*

> [Anyone who does not acknowledge those who control the world and yet wants to poach in their territory risks untimely death . . . But however firmly those women {the *àjé*} support a person, such person must continue to be cool-headed and respectful, for those women value respectfulness a lot.][14]

Yáwọ́ọrẹ́'s action – flaying the deer and spreading its skin out in the open – is seen by the *àjé* as arrogant exhibitionism. The woman, confident of the justness of her petition, first approaches Ọláifá Àdìgún, the Olúọ́dẹ (Head of hunters) of the village, advising him to call Yáwọ́ọrẹ́ to order.[15] Having eventually sought and found the hunter, the woman reproaches him:

> *Lóòtọ́ lọ p'ẹran. A sì fún ọ pa ni. Kí ló dé t'ọọ wá n fi awọ rẹ̀ sóò? Kí ló dé t'ọọ wá lọ rèé kan awọ rẹ̀ m̀'ta gbangba? Sé ò n se gààrù nù-un pé ìwọ l'ọ p'ẹran? Sé'wọ lọ p'ẹran ni àb'aa fún ọ pa? Ọ ọ́ mọ́ pè awọ t'óo gbéé'bẹ̀hun, aṣọ tiwa lo fi nhàn fún gbogbo ayé hun?*

> [I know you killed a deer. But you did because *we* wanted you to. Now why do you show off with its skin? Why did you spread it out, pegged to the ground outside? You sure want to show the whole world that you it was that killed the animal. Were you the one who actually killed the animal or *we* gave it to you? Don't you know spreading out the hide in the open that way is exposing *our* clothing to the mundane world?][16]

Yáwóọré, at this point, resorts to the hunter's regular line about Ògún, the hunter's deity, being the killer and the culprit. The woman boldly rejects the hunter's claim: '*Ògún kọ́, a yọ̀nda ẹ̀ fún ọ ni o*' [*We*, not Ògún, allowed you to kill it]. Dazed and mortified, the hunter submits by prostrating and apologising. He promptly removes the skin and takes it into the house.[17]

The forest spirit sometimes ranks as formidable as the hunter's own deity. In the narrative of Olúfẹ́mi Àjàó Agbérinmì of Tọ́lá village, Ìdó Local Government, Oyo State, the hunter, having invoked the deity to no avail, is pressed into seeking a peaceful resolution.[18] Agbérinmì shoots a duiker in the Forest of Daramola. Though mortally wounded, the duiker struggles to a nearby *ọ̀bọbọ̀* tree, on whose trunk a door appears, opens, admits the wounded animal, closes and disappears. The hunter, in whose full gaze all this has happened, immediately understands that he has been checkmated by the tree-spirit. Angry at having hunted all night, only to lose his kill to a miserly dryad, the hunter is determined to beat the spirit into submission. In vain, he curses and casts a spell of atrophy on the tree. Once more, the door to the tree appears and opens. This time, the spirit comes out and confronts the hunter:

S'óo rí gbogbo ìgbìyànjú ẹ pátápátá, kò leè sisẹ́. Kí ló dé? S'ólè ni ọ́ ni? . . .
'Hun t'ó n gbé é lọ, ìwọ l'ó n sìn í? Ó d'ij'óo t'óo gbé èèrí wá fún wọn.

[All your efforts are bound to fail. What do you want, you thief? Are you the owner of the animal you want to go with? Are you the one feeding them?]

At this point, Agbérinmì also tries the 'Ògún-killed-it' line. The humorous spirit retorts with '*Eb'Ógùn ní n sin ẹran; k'Ògún ọ́ maa gbé e lọ ọ̀*' [Oh, since Ògún it is that owns the animal, let Ògún come for it then]. Thus beaten in the battle of strength and wits, the hunter apologises and offers the spirit a hand of friendship. The spirit accepts the offer, but first instructs the hunter to go to town and buy him a packet of sugar as a mark of friendship. The spirit, after taking delivery of the sugar, later releases the shot duiker to the hunter. He further promises the hunter that whenever he plans to celebrate any important occasion and therefore needs meat:

Máa mú páálí súgà kan, máa wá s'ìdí émi igi ọ̀bọbọ́. T'ọ́ bá d'alẹ́, gbé'ná à
rẹ. Ìdí igi yìí, o ó yin ìbọn, ọ ọ́ pa ẹtu kan n'bẹ̀. Bánkà ni.

[Come with a packet of sugar to me the *ọ̀bọbọ̀* tree. Then, take your hunter's light the following night and come to the tree. You will surely shoot and kill a duiker under it. I assure you.]

Not all the antagonists, however, are successfully won over by the hunter's solicitation. The narrative of Akínwándé Akíntáyọ̀ of Àjóyìnbọn village, Ẹgbẹ́dá Local Government, Oyo State, illustrates such an unresolved impasse in the hunter-spirit relation.[19] It also diverges in its presentation of the antagonist not as owner but as parents of the animals. Akíntáyọ̀, the Olúọ́de of Àjóyìnbọn, is hunting with his friend in the Forest of Àlùgbọ́ when he shoots and kills a monitor lizard. The monitor lizard is among certain classes of animals, including certain human beings, who have the potential of becoming '*iwin* [spirit]' as they advance in age. For example, when the deer carries the hornets' nest in its antlers and barks instead of bleating, or the cobra grows crest and crows like a cock, or the python grows a pair of horns and simulates rainbow, the animal is believed to have attained with age some of the super-animal power that situates it in the realm of the spirits. The monitor that Akíntáyò shoots and kills is evidently in this category: it has aged so much that it has no toes on any of its legs. The hunters hide the lizard and continue with their expedition, planning to pick it on their way back home.

But as they return to retrieve the game, they find an old woman waiting. She charges at them:

> *Ẹ mà l'áyà a! Ẹ tùn padà wá. Ẹ dù'ò nà, ij'òo l'áwa wáá ba yìn n'ígboro yín?*
> *Ẹ sì tún l'áyà, ẹ tún wá, ẹ sì wá pa mí l'ọ́mọ. Aáh, ẹẹ̀ daa o.*

> [Oh, what insolence! You still have the guts to come back. Wait a minute, how many times have *we* intruded in your matters, you humans? Yet you came so boldly and killed *my child*. Oh, you are wicked indeed.]

As the hunters retreat in confusion, having failed to convince the old woman that they killed only a lizard and not a child, she puts a curse on them: however hard they probe the forest, they would never shoot to kill. It was only after months of unsuccessful hunting that the men start to take the woman's pronouncement seriously. They consult the *babaláwo* who reveals to them that '*ẹni tó jù wọ́n lọ n ní n bá wọn ọ́ jà*' [s/he who is stronger than them is at war with them]. To revert the jinx, the priest prescribes a sacrifice to Ògún. Only after the sacrifice are the hunters able to kill.

Domestic matters, too, can play themselves out in the bush (Leach 2000). A vindictive *àjẹ́* woman, still seething from a hunter's offence, may show up in form of strange deer, bent on killing the hunter. By shooting the male of a mating deer-couple, the hunter may have shot his wife's lover. This acknowledgement of 'consubstantiality' (Leach 2000:582) between the tame Self and the wild Other informs the Yoruba hunter's admonition that the hunter conduct himself honourably at home. One hunter sees this bush-home symmetry in terms of human interpersonal relation:

> the hunter kills in the village before leaving for the bush; that is, you must
> be correct to your family at home and to those you live with; if you are not
> correct with those in the village you will not kill in the bush (Leach 2000:83).

In the narrative of Yèkíni Iyìọlá Aróyèhún of Ilé Ogbó, Òṣun State, the protagonist rudely dismisses a woman who wants to buy his first kill of the day.[20] Granted, Aróyèhún already has a guaranteed sale from a meat seller whom he does not want to disappoint, but the hunter's rude dismissal of the woman so much exercises her that she threatens to 'deal with him.' The woman confronts the hunter in form of a duiker. When the hunter sights and fires at it, the barrel of his gun bursts, injuring him. But the animal is also hit. As the animal falls, the offended woman also falls into a sickness that ends in fatality. The narrative connects the two incidents as it closes: on her hospital deathbed, eighteen pellets of the same sizes and number as the one fired at the duiker are extracted from the woman's side, the very point where the hunter had aimed and shot at the duiker.

Agboọlá Alájáníbọn Dẹ́tunhà of Dáli village, Olúyọ̀lé Local Government of Oyo State, confronts the *àjẹ́* for a different reason.[21] Sàfúrátù, the *àjẹ́* character in the narrative, has made some advances to the hunter. When he spurns her, she boils with anger and a resolve to either compel the hunter to have her or destroy him altogether. She also manifests herself in form of a duiker. Dẹ́tunhà's duiker, however, comes with a special portent: it is white. Yoruba hunters know that duikers are not white, but should instead be reddish, with dashes of white. An albino duiker is therefore at least rare, if not impossible. Despite this ominous portent, Dẹ́tunhà shoots and kills the duiker. He nevertheless takes the precaution of sharing the meat among the people, rather than consuming it all himself. This is a popular device among Yoruba hunters hoping to undermine evil aimed at them in form of animal. Rather than deflecting the evil to those who consume it, the action is thought to neutralise it. With Dẹ́tunhà having accordingly shared the white duiker's meat round the village, Sàfúrátù falls ill. When she appears to be dying, she confesses that she had tried to enchant the hunter with the white duiker. She does not, however, actually die. An Ògún àjọbọ, a communal worship of the deity, is organized on her behalf. About 15 pellets fired at the duiker are recovered from her breast.

In the narrative of Ràsákì Àlàó Adúpẹ̀ of Kúseélá village, Ẹgbẹ́dá Local Government, Oyo State, the protagonist also rebuffs the solicitation of an unnamed woman.[22] Having spurned the woman, Adúpé has set off a conflict. The woman's proxy in this conflict is a civet. The civet, after being shot, charges at the hunter and almost bites him, but the hunter finishes the creature off with a blow from a machete just in time. At that point the hunter is struck dumb; rashes break out on his body. Respite only comes through his father, with whom he is hunting, who applies some medication that relieves him. As the animal is gutted, an *ọ̀pẹ̀lẹ̀*, a major instrument used in *ifá* divination, is found in the civet's stomach. Both the hunter and the *àjẹ́* antagonist emerge from the conflict with neither bowing to the other. But much later, when the woman dies, seven holes that other hunters swear are healed bullet wounds are found on her side. In respect to that night of the civet, Adúpé claims, 'Àhàyá méje náà n'mo sì e k'ìbon l'álé ojó náà' [And my gun was loaded that night with seven pellets].

In the largely amoral world of the Yoruba hunter, in which the hunter may choose to have a love affair with the wife of a non-hunter, it is a sin for the non-hunter to have such affair with the hunter's wife, or to contemplate taking her for a wife. It is even more abominable for a hunter to have an affair with the wife of a fellow hunter. The following *ìjálá* lines performed by Akíntáyọ̀ are revealing:[23]

> *Kèé se pé k'ódę ọ́ má fębìn'in ééyán lá n wì*
> *Èyin ẹ sá ti má f'ébìn'in ọdẹ*
> *Ẹ mọ̀ ọ́ níwà ọdẹ, ẹ dà á s'ódẹ lá'a*
> *Ẹnìkan là á kọ̀'wà à'bàjẹ́ fún, ọdẹ ẹ̀'lú ù'Bàdàn*
> *Torí ẹni tọ́ fębìnrin ọdẹ ò jìnà s'íkú*
> *Ikú ò jìnà s'éni ọdẹ bá gbà l'óbìnrin*
> *Tor'éni ọdẹ bá pa bí ọ̀ bá fi kú*
> *Oko o rẹ̀ yíó d'ìgbòrò.*

> [There is nothing wrong about the hunter taking your wife
> But you never take the hunter's wife
> The hunter's weakness is flirtation, just forgive him
> It is noble for one to forgive the other, oh hunter of Ibadan
> For whoever took the hunter's wife is not far away from death
> And death is not far away from he whose wife the hunter has taken
> For whomever the hunter tried to kill and is not dead
> His whole business goes to ruin.]

The narrative of Bándélé Ọlọjẹdẹ of Ìta Màyá, Òkè Àdó, Ibadan, further illustrates the enormity of the love triangle involving the hunter's wife.[24] Bándélé and Bámgbóyè, both hunters, are friends. The narrative establishes that the two are intimate through the preliminary detail that they hunt together. This detail is intended to show the mutual trust between them. Even as a hunter may participate in an expedition with other hunters, including his sworn adversary, virtually none would hunt with his enemy in a two-man party. Equally, the hunter's wife (name not given) is portrayed as the hunter's consort who '*wo 'lé dè mí*' [held fort for me] whenever the hunter is not at home. The narrative then focuses on the two relationships. Bándélé, during a solo expedition in the Forest of Fátùkẹ́, sights a pair of mating deer. Among the Yoruba hunters, there is a belief that whenever the animals of the antelope family mate in the full glare of the hunter, it is a portent that the hunter's wife is unfaithful. It is also believed that the hunter is at liberty to do to the mating pair whatever he wants to happen to the unfaithful wife and her lover. Bándélé shoots the male deer dead; the female escapes with a bullet wound. At home, Bándélé meets his wife writhing in pain. Word also comes that morning that his best friend, Bámgbóyè, is seriously ill. If the audience is uncertain about the complicity of Bámgbóyè and the hunter's wife, the doubt clears as the narrative closes. As the wife's illness worsens, Bándélé calls in the *babaláwo* and the elders who, after a sacrifice of four goats, reveal to the hunter that the wife had been having an affair. During the medication and ritual that follow, six pieces of shrapnel fall out from the woman's body. Bámgbóyè, who has since taken to bed, complaining of having been shot in his dream, also confesses at the point of death to having an affair with Bándélé's wife.

Familiarisation and defamiliarisation

The hunter's translation of the forest's alternative reality aspires to be contemporary with the reality of the human world. In their narratives, old hunters sometimes portray the spirits as addicted to *aásà*, a tobacco stimulant. The Balódè of Ṣakí, cited in Chapter 5, considers the substance a useful item in brokering a favourable deal with the spirits.[25] However, *aásà* is no longer a fashionable stimulant with the younger generation. The spirit in the narrative of Agbérinmì, a hunter of about 35, therefore requests a packet of sugar.[26] Whereas the dancing porcupines in one of the narratives of old Jòògún Àlàdé are dressed in traditional *etù* attire, one of the giant rats in the narrative of Rábíù Òjó, performed by Akíntáyò on Odè Akoni, puts on an American shirt.[27] In the narrative of Àkámóòpèkùn, a dead woman turned deer transforms back into a beautiful woman and '*ó gbé bááàgì ló'ó, ó kó òòka s'ówó, ó fi sèéèní órùn, ó tún d'irun rè l'óndodo*' [she carries a handbag, puts rings on her fingers, wears a necklace and spots a very beautiful hairstyle].[28]

At the same time, however, the hunter also portrays the Other in a manner that rattles the pedestrian sensibility of the non-hunter audience. For example, in the narrative of Músílíù Àlàgbé Fìríàáríkú performed by Akíntáyò, the narrator exclaims: '*Igbó Oníwòrò yí, enìkan ìí dè'gbé loo'bè k'ó bó o. Igbó burúkú gbáà tó l'ágbára gbáà ni*' [No hunter goes to the Forest of Oníwòrò and returns. It is evil and indeed very malevolent].[29]

But whereas some narrators evoke awe through such description, others merely downplay the Other's formidability, a narrative device that proves equally successful in eliciting awe. Schechner (1993) notes a similar wilful downplaying of importance in the Wahema, the Passion and Resurrection performance among the Yaqui of New Pascua, Arizona, Mexico. In this performance, the local audience is not particularly absorbed in watching the drama; their occasional sidelong glances at the Wahema reinforce the ordinariness of the carnival to the average Yaqui.

[The] Yaqui way is to observe by means of glancing, avoiding intense frontal gazing . . . [Those] who press in hardest, most anxious to 'see it all' are usually outsiders (Schechner 1993:108).

In the extreme, the Yaqui pursue their abnegation of absolute audience involvement by forbidding the tourists to record the performance. The result is that the very spectatorship that the tradition seems to downplay is, ironically, encouraged; the seemingly disinterested local audience only creates another level of performance for the curious, remote foreign audience.

In much the same way, the radio broadcast of the narrative of Táníátù Akínkúnmi Akéwejè paints the forest and its weirdness in such dull colours, with such familiarity with the Other, that his portrait produces more excitement than would hyperbole.[30] He describes his dialogue with the river in such ordinary terms that it is only when another dialogue between the hunter, on the one hand, and the antagonist (àràbà and rock), on the other, ensues that the bewildered audience asks whether river, tree or rock actually speaks. In the same manner, Akéwejè treats his initial failure to see the invisible deer so matter-of-factly that a listener thinks he must have meant that the animal is covered by foliage. It is only when the question is asked and the narrator clarifies that *Kóóko 'ò bò ó, but mi 'ò rí i* [No it wasn't covered by the foliage, but I did not see it] and *'ọta hóró kan 'ò sòfò lára a rẹ̀* [all the bullets found their target] that listeners realise in awe that the protagonist is faced with a deer that is both invisible and proofed against gunshot.

In the narrative of Bilaminu Babátúndé Ajíjààgùn of Alùgbín village, Ẹgbẹ̀dà, Ibadan, the hunter, during a night hunt, stops under a palm tree to drink the wine left for him by his palm wine tapper. He starts in surprise when someone calls him but is later relieved when he identifies the intruder: *'Òrọ̀ ọ 'gi tiẹ̀ ni. Kíní a n bọ̀ wá se níi 'ín?'* [Oh, it's only a tree spirit. What's his business here?]. Treating one of the most formidable antagonists in the hunters' narratives so casually enhances the hunter's portrait as a veteran in dealing with danger. It is the same casual attitude that gives Fagunwa's hunters, especially Akara-ogun, prominence. Though the entirety of the hunters' narratives are an exercise in making the weird Other comprehensible to man, the above represents the consummate immersion of man in the Same-Other dialogic complex with such depth that the audience can only marvel.

Truth, mythmaking and management of credibility risk

In the hunter's narrative, reality is so flexible that a character may step into a mirror and hug his own image. The flexible texture of the narrated reality makes the composition look so easy that it could all have been total fiction or, more dismissively put, a lie. The hunter narrator is apprehensive that his mythmaking stands the risk of outright dismissal as a thought-up tale. Moreover, the performer must take responsibility for the success or failure of his performance. Standard exists, however tacit, in every culture with which the performer is expected to either conform – or diverge creatively from.

Among the Yoruba, for example, the periodic *'Hẹn'* [Yes] refrain from co-*babaláwo* to a *babaláwo* performing the *ìyẹrẹ̀* is an indication that his lines are accurate. If he falters, he is stopped, and another *babaláwo* is made to continue the performance. It is by 'this rigid insistence on the correct recital of the *Ifá* texts [that] *Ifá* priests have made it almost impossible for spurious passages to appear in *Ifá* literary corpus' (Abimbola 1976:15–16). Yankah (1985) notes that the performer takes risk in every work he undertakes. If today, the consequence is not as dire as among the precolonial Akan, who beheaded their faltering *apae* poets (Yankah 1983), performers nevertheless muster all possible devices to endear their performance to the audience.

Akíntáyọ̀ thus regularly appeals to patriarchy as a means to reinforce the credibility of a claim. For example, to establish the claim that the duiker drinks water with its hooves instead of the mouth, he directs the listeners to confirm this account from *'àwọn àgbàlagbà'* [the elders]. In the narrative of Kọ̀bọmọjẹ́ Àlàdé, as the jingles of the aerial spirit come closer to the hunter, the narrator pauses to check in with the bewildered listener, assuring him:

> *N ọ̀ gbọdọ̀ purọ́ o; ọdẹ n'ìran baba à mi. Ọmọ Oròówùsì n'Íbàdàn ni mòó se . . . N'ìlù ú 'Bàdàn, ọdẹ ni bàbá à mi, wọ́n sì l'óókọ.*

> [I tell no lie; hunting runs in my paternal line. I am of the Oròówùsì family in Ibadan . . . In the city of Ibadan, my father was a well-known hunter, and very reputable too.][31]

Ògúnkúnlé Òjó tells the story of his master, Ògúnlékè Ògúnòṣun. His third-person perspective suggests the possibility that his account might not be as accurate as the original protagonist's might have been. The narrator therefore reminds the audience of his status as a minor character in the narrative: *'N ọ̀ gbọ́ 'ẹwífúnmi'; èmi Òjó ọdẹ n bẹ n'bẹ̀ n'jọ́ náà'* [This is no hearsay; I Òjó the hunter was present there that day].[32]

When the antagonist transforms into a buffalo, Òjó, in order to shake off the audience's incredulity, repeats *'N ọ̀ gbọ́ 'ẹwífúnmi'; l'ẹ́gbẹ̀ẹ́ 'leé bàbá Adémọ́lá ló ti di ẹranko,. . . lára Òkèè 'Gbàdì'* [It is no hearsay; it was by Ademola's father's house that she transformed into an animal, . . . beside Ìgbàdì Hill]. By thus placing the event in a contemporary, familiar environment, Òjó mitigates the risk of incredibility that comes not only with his narrative perspective, but also with the unusual reality that the story deals with.

Similarly, the display of memorabilia from the hunter's supernatural encounters is an effort to enhance credibility. Using the example of a narrator identified as Sade, Oyegoke (1994) writes on testimony in the Nigerian churches as a genre of narrative performance. In order to convince her audience of the veracity of her account, Sade displays a number of items used in the art of witchcraft as she evokes her 'unholy' days as a witch. In the same way, Rabiu Òjó adorns the costume of his *egúngún* with the hide of the animal half of the half-woman-half-civet of his narrative (see Appendix C). He encourages the audience to look out for it the next *egúngún* season. The hunter Ásìmíyù Ògúndépò Pabíẹkùn shows the gourdlet he wins in the encounter with the spirit owner of the duiker to the radio host who in turn describes it to the listeners (see Plate 3.2). Moses Ògúnwálé similarly displays the *atọ́* and the *adọ́* gourdlets of his narrative (see Plate 3.1). Lawal Ògúntúndé, the Balọ́de of Ṣakí, also shows his trophy, in form of a horn of a buffalo that almost kills him, the hunter-hero of his narrative (see Plate 1.9). In the same way that the mythmaker of modern theatre uses costumes and props to suspend his audience's disbelief, the hunter-narrator employs memorabilia. In the hunter's case, he wants to annul disbelief altogether.

Language and the portrait of anOther world

The hunter's way with words promotes the image of a narrator with a third eye. His vocabulary is peculiar in a manner that defamiliarises even the known world before an audience of non-hunters. For example, when the hunter simply says that '*mo t'ọwọ́ bọ gbérí*' [I put hand in my cloak], it is implied that he does so to take out a charm. In the narrative of Músílíù Àlàgbé Fìríàáríkú, the narrator says, '*Mọ wá t'ọwọ́ b'àpò, mọ fà'bínú yọ*' [I put hand in my pocket and brought out a fit of anger] (see Appendix A). His interlocutor adds '*Ẹ t'ọwọ́ bọ gbérí?*' [You put your hand in the *cloak*?] evidently to situate '*àpò*' [pocket] in a more 'hunterly' parlance, namely, '*gbérí*' [cloak]. Ameringun takes the cue and repeats the statement in more figural '*Mọ t'ọwọ́ bọ'kùn, mọ fà'bínú yọ*' [I put hand in my *gut* and brought out a fit of anger]. The hunters refer to many other things in such figural terms that the non-hunters are always compelled to ask for clarification. Some of these terms are listed in Table 4.1:

Table 4.1: Some terms the hunters use

Word/expression	Hunter	Non-hunter
gun	*làsà*, *ògún*, *bájínátù*, *àtùpà Ògún* [Ògún's lamp]	*ìbọn*
machete	*Ígannà*	*àdá*
pellet	*ẹyin eyelé* [pigeon's egg]	*ọta*
'the barrel of the gun bursts'	'*ìbọn kú*' ['the gun dies']	'*ìbọn fọ́*'
'the animal has died'	'*ẹran pako*'; '*ẹran sùn* ['the animal has slept']	'*ẹran kú*'
lion	*ajá nlá* [the big dog], *gúnnú*, *jàntá*	*kìnnìún*
deer	*ẹran pupa* [red animal]	*ìgalá*, *àgbọnrín*
grasscutter	*ẹmọ́* [rat]	*òyà*
magical power, charm	*aájò*, *mátàgbàmọ́lẹ̀* [that which does not let the elder suffer insult]	*Òògùn*

The sense of being in another world suggested by the hunter's encounter is further strengthened by the evocation of distance. The hunter-narrator not only sometimes sets his story far away from the place of its performance, but also stresses the relatively long period over which the expedition takes place. In the narrative of Aṣípa Oláògún of Ọ̀jẹ́ Owódé, set in 1946, the Ọlọjẹẹ, the *ọba* of Ọ̀jẹ́ Owódé, has recruited Ògúnjìmí, the narrator's elder brother, and another unidentified hunter to take a white man on what seems to be a surveillance tour of some forests. Oláògún describes the journey:

> *Wọ́n lo ọgbọ̀n ọjọ́ àti ijọ́ méje, wọ́n wá fi n yí igbó. N'gbà a wọ́n bẹ̀rẹ̀ láti Ijù Apá, wọ́n wá gb'ọnẹ̀ Odò Ìkẹ̀rẹ̀ lọ́nẹ̀ẹ̀'Sẹ́yìn, wọ́n lọ sí Àbàtà Ẹ̀pà. Wọ́n ti Àbàtà Ẹ̀pà, wọ́n lọ sí Igbó Ìmẹ̀rì. Láti Igbó Ìmẹ̀rì, wọ́n padà lọ sí Odò Òkòkò. Láti Odò Òkòkò, wọ́n lù ú lọ sí apá ọtún, wọ́n fi já Òkè Gòngo. Lẹ́yìn ìgbà néẹ́ [kàkà] kí wọn ó fi yọ s'ílùú, wọ́n wá jáde sí Ìpàpó.*

[They spent thirty and seven days, going round the forests. They started from Wilderness of Apá and went through the road to Ìkẹ̀rẹ̀ River by Ìsẹ́yìn to Ẹ̀pà Swamp. From Ẹ̀pà Swamp, they went to the Forest of Ìmẹ̀rì. From the Forest of Ìmẹ̀rì, they returned to Òkòkò River. From Òkòkò River, they came out from the right flank and emerged at the Heights of Gòngo. Thereafter, instead of returning home, they came out at Ìpàpó.][33]

In the narrator's detailing of the hunters' journey, the sense of other-worldliness created through such unfamiliar destinations as Apá, Èpà, Ìmèrì, Òkòkò and Gòngo is further enhanced by references to widely known places like Ìséyìn, Ìkèrè and Ìpàpó, all of which are too distant from Òjé to be travelled to on foot. Akíntáyò similarly describes the long trek to the Forest of Ìkèrè, home to a half-beast-half-man misanthrope, in his performance of the narrative of Múdàsírù Òjó Apààrà of Ìméléke village, Oyo West Local Government:

> B'áa bá kúrò n'ílùú Òyó, t'áa dé'Gbó Olóògùn, t'áa kojá, t'áa rìnrìn i wákàtí kan pèlú esè rínrìn, aá kan odò tí won ó pè ní Òówé. T'áa bá dá Òówé kojá, aá rìnrìn i wákàtí kan, aá kan odò tí won n pè ní Àálá. T'áa bá dé odò tí won n pè ní Àálá, aá rìnrìn i wákàtí kan, aá dèé odò tí won n pè ní Alègò. T'áa bá gba Alègò, t'áa bá gùn ú s'ókè gàràrà, a bó s'ára dáàmù nù-un: dáàmù yí ni won n pè ní Ìkèrè Daàmù.

> [When you set out on foot from Òyó town, going through Olóògùn Forest, after walking for about one hour, you get to a river called Òówé. After crossing Òówé over, you walk for another hour and get to another river called Àálá. From Àálá, another one-hour trek takes you to another river called Alègò. When you then pass by Alègò and go further up, you get near the dam called Ìkèrè Dam.][34]

It is worth noting that these descriptions are offered by third-person narrators. Just as in the third-person performance of the *ofò* cited earlier, the two narrators' descriptions of the landscapes are designed to demonstrate their equal familiarity with those parts. As with Akara-ogun, the implied performer of Olowo-aye's narrative, it is by being thus picturesque and 'accurate' that the narrator subtly inscribes his own knowledge as a hunter in his performance of the story of another. The sense of distance and a long journey is conveyed not only in the evocation of a long trek, but also through setting the hunter's story far away from either the hunter's home or the place of the narrative's performance. In the narrative of Kòbomojé Àlàdé, the hunter goes from Ibadan to hunt in Ìséyìn. In the narrative of Àpémò Kínche, he comes from Hounkoko, Republic of Benin.[35] Though in these two narratives, the hunter-protagonists actually live in the settings of the stories, the distance of these fictive settings from Ibadan, the place of the present performance, nevertheless enhances a sense of other-worldliness.

In the hunter's encounter, hierarchies and representations rupture and are also permutated. The hunter, once a human conqueror of the wild, is beaten into submission and becomes a fugitive. The bush-homefront borders, sustained in his narrative defamiliarisation, also collapse as a wife and a cuckold become deer and a buffalo becomes a wife. In a world where the definition of Self and Other are thus plagued with uncertainty, the hunter relies not only on strength, but also on diplomacy and humility.

Notes

1. *Ọdẹ́tẹ̀dó*, n.d.

2. *Ọdẹ Akọni*, 28/09/2003.

3. Personal interaction, 11/02/2007.

4. *Ọdẹ Akọni*, 24/12/2006.

5. *Ọdẹ Akọni*, 10/12/2006.

6. Personal interaction, 07/10/2007.

7. Personal interaction, 23/05/2007.

8. *Ọdẹ Akọni*, 05/11/2003.

9. *Ọdẹ Akọni*, 05/11/2003.

10. *Ọdẹ́tẹ̀dó*, n.d.

11. Personal interaction, 14/08/2005.

12. *Ọdẹ Akọni*, 24/07/2005.

13. Interview, 16/12/2006.

14. Interview, 17/04/2007.

15. *Ọdẹ Akọni*, 24/07/2005.

16. Personal interaction, 14/08/2005.

17. *Ọdẹ Akọni*, 24/07/2005.

18. *Ọdẹ Akọni*, 05/08/2007.

19. *Ọdẹ Akọni*, 08/05/2005.

20. *Ọdẹ Akọni*, 17/09/2003.

21. *Ọdẹ Akọni*, 20/02/2005.

22. Personal interaction, 20/02/2005.

23. *Ọdẹ Akọni*, 29/04/2007.

24.   Personal interaction, 29/05/2007.

25.   Personal interaction, 27/02/2007.

26.   *Ọdẹ Akọni*, 05/08/2007.

27.   *Ọdẹ Akọni*, 20/06/2004.

28.   *Ọdẹ Akọni*, 06/03/2005.

29.   *Ọdẹ Akọni*, 01/08/2004.

30.   *Ọdẹ Akọni*, 13/06/2004.

31.   Personal interaction, 07/10/2007.

32.   Personal interaction, 11/02/2007.

33.   Personal interaction, 16/1220/06.

34.   *Ọdẹ Akọni*, 04/07/2004.

35.   Personal interaction, 02/05/2006. Kínche currently lives in Ìgbínjẹ village, Ilé Ogbó, Ọsun State.

5

The Hunter on the Airwaves

Introduction

The broadcast media of radio and, to some extent, television have given prominence to the hunter's narrative. This chapter discusses the implication of these new expressive outlets for the ethic of silence with which the hunter is associated. The unequal performance of the two media is also examined in the light of the capitalist economy that empowers and/or disempowers them as an agent of cultural production.

The ethic of silence and the imperative of narrativity

In this book I have argued that there is art to non-formalised expressive spaces such as conversation and speech. The hunter's narratives oppose, in a manner of speaking, the consciously performative stances exemplified by such normative types as the Yoruba *àló*, the Kalabari *ikaki*, the Zulu *izibongo*, and the Akan *Anansesɛm*. For a number of reasons, the Yoruba hunter, even in the thick of a narrative performance, acknowledges the virtue in taciturnity and total silence: '*Tí ọdẹ bá ro ìṣé, ti ọdẹ bá ro ìyà, t'ó bá p'ẹran, kò níí f'ẹnìkankan*' [If the hunter takes stock of all his adversities, he would share his kill with no one]. The word *rò* in the above maxim more readily suggests 'take stock of', or, more literally, 'think of'. But it also translates as 'recount' or 'narrate'. To narrate therefore is to highlight the hunter's experience as an individual, consequently running the risk of severing the umbilical that joins the hunter and his community. In this sense, narrative individuates to the point that it threatens to alienate an organ from the entire system.

In another sense, the weird reality that is the hunter's narrative challenges contemporary perception of the hunter and his craft. This potential is inscribed in a proverb: '*Òòjó n'iyì ọdẹ afifilàperin*' [The glory of the hunter that killed an elephant with a mere swat of his cap lasts but for a day]. The full interpretation is realised in the unspoken half of the proverb, which supposes that after the immediate and spontaneous admiration of the hero-hunter, he is deemed dangerous, and avoided. A phobia of the hunter's craft also runs the possibility of threatening his business. The consumer may not find a diet of half-human civet, or a deer that previously was a Fulani woman, appetising (see appendices B and C). This is primary argument of those opposed to the explicit narrative performance of the hunter's experience through broadcast media. On 2 October 2005, a woman, identified as Ìyá Àmẹ́ẹ̀dì, the chairperson of the bush meat sellers in Ibadan, brought a petition to the authorities of the Broadcasting Corporation of Oyo State (BCOS) asking the producers of *Ọdẹ Akọni* to either tone down the gory details or to remove them altogether. Coming from a family of hunters herself, she reasoned that the disclosure of the weird world from which the animals emerge would discourage consumers. In her appeal, broadcast on the day's edition of the programme, she confessed her total belief in the reality of what the hunters told, but argued that the hunter's experience was best kept secret; that, in her reckoning, was the ethic as inherited and bequeathed by her forefathers.

But the idea that the hunters' narratives have remained secret until the advent of modern broadcasting is palpably false. Even in the most conservative of villages with the most taciturn hunters, the ancient impulse to tell stories creates seepages through which they leak out. With a look over his shoulders to ensure that the women and children are out of sight, the hunter, in a discussion with other male adults, may quickly illustrate a point with an account of his experience. For example, in the narrative of Kìlání Alápó, briefly cited in Chapter 4, the narrator declaims that '*àwọn ọdẹ a máa gbé ọ̀rọ̀ ọ' nú*' [hunters are adept at keeping secrets]: he tells no one of the strange deerskin in his custody – *except his babalawo and a couple of friends.*[1] It is widely known therefore in every community which hunter once took a buffalo-turned-woman for a wife, or which one was once beaten up by a gang of ghosts.

One popular resolution of the quandary implicit in the hunter's ethic of silence contra the imperative of storytelling is that the ethic does not totally proscribe narrativity. This interpretation holds that the hunter may *tell*, but that he must be careful and selective in his choice of audience and details. The ethic, as such, sets up the hunter as a mythmaker. The need to exclude 'sensitive' details from his narrative demands circumspection, considering the spontaneous nature of its performance. But the ethic of silence sometimes becomes a device that imbues the narrative with additional value. The awareness that the listener is witness to a guarded secret creates curiosity and ensures attentiveness.

At the end of the twentieth century, the imperatives of economy and mass communication technology further and decisively breached the illusion of silence with which the hunter's story had been associated. First, in the early 1990s, in Yoruba-speaking parts of Nigeria, the content of broadcast radio performances shifted from excerpts of fictional literary works to extempore narration of events considered and presented as real-life experiences. Narratives of such supernatural themes as the *àjẹ́* afflicting a man, or a man's visit to the town of the dead, started to enjoy a popular audience. Kọ́lá Ọláwuyì's *Ìrírí Ayé* and Kọ́lá Olóòtú's *Òwúyẹ́* belong in this genre. According to Bremond (1996), the index of the success of a narrative is not just the sum of the aesthetic devices deployed in its performance but, significantly, the volume of attention it generates. These radio series were so popular in the last half of the 1990s that many of their presenters disengaged from their salaried employment with the media houses to establish some kind of independent practice; they solicited for advertisements on their programmes and paid for the airtime from the proceeds.

Nigerian advertisers also value popularity. They know that certain programmes command a greater audience than others and therefore understand the benefits of promoting their products on those that attract the most listeners. These radio programmes, hugely popular among the Yoruba-speaking population, thereby became a popular choice for advertisers. It was the stark prospect of ensuring better income through the independent broadcast of such narrative programmes that naturally weaned many broadcasters from their salaried jobs. The success of Kọ́lá Ọláwuyì after his dismissal from Radio Nigeria, Ibadan, allayed any immediate fear of the commercial failure of such independent projects. At the time of his death in 2007, the broadcaster had built a viable business empire in its own right that presented narrative programmes on no less than four radio stations and three television stations.

In March 2000, *Ọdẹ Akọni*, the hunters' narrative series, debuted on the amplitude modulation (am) band of the BCOS. Since then, it has been broadcast every Sunday between 21:00 and 23:00. Kọ́lá Akíntáyọ̀, the presenter, a hunter himself, describes his vision for the programme:

> 'Hun tó mú èmi bẹ̀rẹ̀ ètò Ọdẹ Akọni ni wípé ètò ìsẹ̀se kọ̀ wọ́pọ̀ lóríi réédíò mọ́. Bíi kí wọ́n ọ sọ p'áwọn fẹ́ sọ ìrírí ayé, kí wọn ọ́ máa mú osó, kí wọn ọ́ máa m'ájẹ̀ẹ́; lágbájá l'óhun ọ́ pa lágbájá, o sì ti fẹ́ẹ́ pa á o [àti bẹ́ẹ̀ bẹ́ẹ̀ lọ] ló pọ̀ l'óri aféfẹ́. Mo wáá wò ó pé àwọn ohun t'ójú u tèmí maa n rí tí n bá d'ẹ̀gbẹ́ lọ, ó tó ìrírí fún ará ìlú.

> [What made me start *Ọdẹ Akọni* was the dearth of indigenous cultural radio programmes. There had been preponderance of {narrative} programmes in which people were indicted as wizards, witches, murderers {and so on}. So, I reflected on some of the things I myself experienced as a hunter during

expeditions and concluded that they were good materials for entertaining the listeners.]

Akíntáyò's indictment of the existing narrative programmes is best understood at the foreground of the belief that most of the Yoruba audience invest in the stories. The audience do not consider the narratives to be fiction but reports of the experiences of identifiable human beings. Narratives usually gain their energy, and thereby their human interest, through conflict. In these existing programmes, the conflict tends to be manifest in such forms as the *àjé* grandmother afflicting the helpless grandchild, or the unholy church pastor who ensures optimum patronage by sealing the soul of the church's congregation in a hermetic talisman jar. Sometimes the broadcasts include the actual people involved narrating from their own points of view. But unlike in most well-wrought fiction, conflicts are not always resolved in the narratives. Indeed, they might even continue into the courts, with the host sometimes being fined for defamation. Akíntáyò's vision of relocating conflict to the forest is therefore consonant with the hunter's calling as a sort of mediator and pacifier. His project intertwines with the hunter's primordial preoccupation of keeping in the wild all that is wild, so that man may be 'correct with his neighbours' (Leach 2000:583).

Many still believe today that the hunter's story would be better not told. When *Ọdẹ Akọni* began to broadcast, there were a number of petitions, culminating in the bush meat sellers' appeal cited above. It was in the midst of this opposition that the radio series began and gradually established itself. Despite opposition from a quarter of the hunters' population, from among whom Akíntáyò had intended to draw performers, the programme continued with no major hitch. According to the presenter: ' *'Hun tó jé kó rọrùn f'émi jù ni 'ípé ọdẹ ni mí . . . Ọpọlọpọ̀ tí mo n gbé wá s'órí ètò gan-an, èmi gan d'ẹ̀gbẹ́ j'ẹlòmíì lọ'* [What made it easy for me was that I am a hunter myself . . . I am, in fact, more experienced than some of the hunters I feature on the programme].

As such, the hunter occurs once more as an innovator, as one who discovers at the cost of breaching the cultural walls from within, exposing himself to a charge of treachery.

One principal factor in Akíntáyò's programme's success is the capitalist economy in which it operates. The show has proved popular, and advertisers support it. Another hunter television discussion programme, *Ọdẹ̀tẹ̀dò*, premiering on BCOS Television in 2003, was less successful. Its main focus was not narrative and, arguably as a result, did not secure the kind of popularity enjoyed by *Ọdẹ Akọni*. It was unceremoniously taken off the air in the middle of 2005.[2] Throughout about three years of its broadcast, it featured no commercial advertisements. In a personal discussion, Lekan Babatunde, the programme's producer, disclosed that the production could not secure a sponsor.

Broadcast on BCOS Television every Thursday between 18:15 and 19:00, *Ọdẹ̀tẹ̀dó* began in 2003 with a little hiccup: occasional programmes that were more commercially attractive to the television authorities were sometimes aired in its place, without any rescheduling of the programme. It will be useful to know that while *Ọdẹ Akọni*, the radio programme – and, of course, many other existing non-hunter narrative series on radio and television – was designed and presented by an independent broadcaster, while *Ọdẹ̀tẹ̀dó* was produced by staff of the BCOS. Independent broadcasters, in Nigerian terms, are non-employees of the media houses; they design their own programmes and literally buy airtime to broadcast these programmes out of the money made from advertisements and sponsorships. It is therefore inferable that independent broadcasters owe their livelihood to the survival of their programmes more than their counterparts in the employ of the media houses do. This factor affects not only the personnel's commitment, but more significantly broadcast programming in line with the very popular taste. *Ọdẹ̀tẹ̀dó* set a lofty and ambitious cultural agenda – in line with the policy of the government that owns the media house – of giving coverage to the entire world of the hunter's world and arts: *ìjálá, ìrèmọ̀jé, ìsípà*, descriptions of forest and wildlife in Yoruba terms, hunters' narratives, and so on. Much of the content of the programme, though entertaining in its own right, is from the public aspects of the Yoruba hunter's world with which at least a quarter of the audience is familiar. Hunters' narratives were also performed on *Ọdẹ̀tẹ̀dó*. However, unlike in the case of *Ọdẹ Akọni* that specifically isolates the narrative and makes other aspects such as *ìjálá* and *ìrèmọ̀jé* subsidiary, *Ọdẹ̀tẹ̀dó* had a more panoramic dimension; narratives were broadcast only in about one out of every three editions, and only as a segment. The popular story-hungry Yoruba audience that consumes not only radio and television narratives, but also local films, are not particularly keen on monitoring such programmes.

Television and radio audiences are largely drawn to contents that take them a little away from the *known* into the *new*. Although, as I pointed out earlier, the hunter's story was not a secret in the absolute sense, it was nevertheless a rarely narrated Yoruba experience. The astute independent broadcaster, whose livelihood depends on the continuity of his programme, profits from this type of rarity; he reconciles his potential with the passion and taste of his prospective audience. *Ọdẹ̀tẹ̀dó*, has been taken of the air again, and maybe for good, while on the other hand, *Ọdẹ Akọni* is assured airtime as long as the advertisement bill is settled. There were, in fact, occasions when the am station ceased transmission and the programme had to be broadcast on the frequency modulation (fm) band.

Schechner (1993:48) says that when 'unofficial culture worms or bullies its way . . . into public outdoor spaces', its need for breath of life might leave it vulnerable to 'capitalism's appetite for profit'. In such situations, the cultural form is not only at the mercy of the capitalist establishment, but is also deliberately redesigned to suit its commercial interests. Cooper (1998:46), drawing from the works of Jean Franco and Victor Beilis, also writes on the exotification of cultural items to generate tourist appeal. For her, the narrative of Amos Tutuola is far more acceptably 'archaic is [sic] that it is steeped in the old ways and tradition: the mother culture of . . . Tutuola is more archaic because it belongs to a tribal society'. It is in this context that writers in the magical realist mode, such as Gabriel Garcia Marquez, are viewed as not just asserting alterity as a form of protest but also as an appeal to popular audiences. Cooper (1998:49) is implying that, even as these writers have successfully adjusted to the postcolonial expressive climate, they do not boast the same type of cultural rootedness exhibited by Tutuola and Fagunwa. The school of thought that says that capitalism distorts postcolonial cultures, represented by Schechner and Cooper, does not seem to recognise the dynamics of renewal, innovation and adaptation built into the indigenous forms themselves. In many Yoruba cultural forms, inlet facilities exist through which the so-called exotic is admitted in permissible mass without effacing the principal essence of the host culture.

As an illustration, consider an experience in the research field for the book. On 27 February 2007, I visited Lawal Ògúntúndé, the Balóde of Ṣakí,[3] to interview him and conduct a group discussion with some of the hunters he mentored. As I turned on the recorder and prepared to ask the first question, about five men came into the living room and stopped the session. They demanded that the patriarch be paid some sort of honorarium before the interview commenced. The old hunter's feeble protest did nothing to hold off the young men. After the fee had been settled and the young men had departed, the old man rationalised the contretemps:

> *B'aa s'òfé Ọló'un ó m'óhun t'ólúwa è ó je wá; b'aa s'owó, Ọló'un ó m'óhun t'ólúwa è ó je wá . . . Gégé bí ohun tí wón wí nì, towótowó néè ni gbogbo nken nîisìínyìí. Ohun t'ee bá gbó l'énuu wa, ó l'eni éyin néè tón lò n wí fún. Wón sì n'íbi t'aa jìyà làá j'oore.*

> [Whether we charged money or not, God would definitely not let us starve . . . But as the men noted, everything has now gone commercial. Whatever you people hear from us, you definitely have some people somewhere you also tell it to. And the saying goes that wherever a man has toiled he should also thrive.]

Even in his acknowledgement that contemporary human relations are rather unpleasantly determined by mercenary interests, the old man means that the hunter, rather than forswear participation, will negotiate and survive it. For him, the culture, of which he is a vendor, is already structured to tolerate and contain such changes without any visible damage to its core. He understands the interview as an item of some commercial value to both the researcher and the hunter. The same commercial principle that runs through the hunter's sale of the bush meat underlies the interview as an exercise in exchange. Lest the researcher think the commercial temper is an entirely modern phenomenon, the clever old man began his discussion on the nature of intercourse between the hunter and 'ǹkęnkíǹkęn [odd things, or spirits]' by pointing at its essentially commercial nature. The hunter-ǹkęnkíǹkęn relation is additionally understood in the old man's reflection as a phenomenon of 'ayé ìjeèló' [the gone old days]: 'L'áyéè 'jeèló, ǹkęnkíǹkęn bí àwọn ànjòọnọ́, wọn a maa fún àwọn baba wa ní nkęn' [In the gone old days, odd things such as the spirits used to give our forefathers 'things'].

The old hunter explained that the hunter of old, as a matter of course, always entered the forest with *aásà* (ground tobacco) as part of his provisions. The item is believed to be a stimulant of high value to the spirits. It is therefore one of the things that the hunter trades for a favour from the spirit. The aspect of commerce is further highlighted by the suggestion of risk. The hunter could be in danger if *ǹkęnkíǹkęn*

> *bá kò ọ́ l'ọ̀nẹ̀, t'ó ní o bùn hun l'áásà mọ, t'óo gbé e le e l'ọ́wọ́ . . ., ó è t'ibẹ̀ bun'lúwa'ẹ̀ l'óògùn daadaa t'ólúwa è nẹ́ẹ̀ ọ́ mọọ fi jẹ'un . . . Àmọ́ t'ólúwa'ẹ̀ ọ̀ bá fi rí áásà nì, ó lè se'lúwa'ẹ̀ lése.*

> [meets you on the way, asks you to spare him some tobacco to chew and you oblige him . . ., he may, as a result, give you a charm from which you will profit . . . But if one does not have the tobacco, he may hurt you.]

In much the same way that the hunter constructs a continuum between bartering and the modern economy, so does Akíntáyò in regard to the radio series. Even as he admits that the hunter's story is public entertainment today because '*ayé ti d'ayé ọ̀làjú*' [modern civilisation has taken over], he nevertheless regards it as '*ètò ìsẹ̀sẹ*' [a primordial indigenous form].

Broadcast media and the 'sin' of narrative reconstruction

The hunter's narrative is broadcast in the evening, at a time of day when the presenter benefits from the eerie ambience of the night to highlight the awesome aspects of his narrative (Okpewho 1983). There are three broad types of radio performance. The first involves the host performing the narrative either in the presence or absence of the guest-hunter and protagonist. In this mode, the hunter merely comes on air at the end of the narrative to affirm the presenter's version and answer telephone calls from the listeners. Though inquiries from callers may warrant that the hunter enlarge certain aspects of the story, his contribution to the performance is often mostly in the form of a brief affirmation or correction rather than in adding a new dynamic perspective to the narrative. In the second mode, the hunter takes charge of the performance of his narrative, moderated by the prompting and queries of the host. In the third, the presenter begins the performance and, midway, brings in the hunter to conclude the story. All three modes of performance commonly feature a sort of audience participation through phone calls at the end of the narrative. When the hunter is present in the studios, he answers the callers' questions.

Many oral performance scholars have made the point that a story twice told is two stories (Finnegan 1970; Okpewho 1983). It may be added that differences and discrepancies do not begin between one version of a narrative and another but, in fact, with differences from the real event and its narrative reconstruction. Since the hunter is often the sole witness to the former, it is not easy to probe this first level of discrepancy between the fabula and the narrative text. The performance of Ásìmíyù Ògúndépò Pabíẹkùn (see Plate 4.1), however, points to the possibility of this kind of slip.[4] The hunter-protagonist in the narrative comes through as skilful and experienced when, upon seeing a pair of eyes far away, reflecting in the dark, he promptly ascertains: '*Ojú yìí, ojú akọ ẹtu nìíì*' [Those were the eyes of a male duiker]. As the struggle between the hunter and the spirit-owner of the animal becomes tense, the narrator says: '*Ìyá ẹran gan l'èyí tí mọ pa yìí, tó j'óbí ẹran*' [The one I had killed was the nanny duiker, mother of the entire herd], negating the earlier claim that the duiker is male. But Pabíẹkùn is a clever narrator. He quickly recalls that he has earlier called the animal male, and promptly dumps that mistake on the antagonist since she is the one who calls it female in the story anyway:

> *Mọ l'ákọ ẹran l'èmí pa. Ó ní akọ tí mọ pa hun, ó l' 'Oò ti mọ wípé òhun ní ngun ìyá ẹran. Kò s'òbúkọ mìí mọ́ nù-ún.*

> [I replied that the one I killed was male. 'Even though it was male,' she said, 'don't you know that is the only stud duiker that mates with the females?']

It is by thus crediting the slip to a character that Pabíẹkùn saves the narrative from this discrepancy.

Whenever the hunter comes on either to perform the last half of the narrative or answer the listeners' calls, the presenter always asks that he point out any discrepancy between '*ohun tó sẹlẹ gan-an*' [what actually happened] and the account he has given so far. The usual response is to affirm with such statement as '*kò s'írọ́ n'bi òkankan n'bẹ̀; b'ó se rí gẹ́lẹ́ n náà lẹ tóka sí hun*' [there is no discrepancy; you narrated it the way it happened].[5] Detail for detail, the radio presenter's attempt to aspire to artistry through embellishment in third-person narration sometimes creates a slightly different picture. In the first-person performance of the narrative of Améringùn, for example, the hunter compares the antagonist spirit's eyes to human fists.[6] Akíntáyò's earlier performance of the same narrative, before the hunter is brought on air, employs a different metaphor:

> Ọdẹ́ fi yé wa wípé ojú ànjọọ̀nú yìí . . . Haà! S'ẹẹ mọ kinní iná rogodo tí wọ́n maá fi sí mọ́tò kó le baà tún rína síi? Ó ní b'ójú àjọọ̀nu hún kọọ̀kan bó se rí nù-un ròɡòdòrogodo. Ó ní n ló sì mọ́lẹ̀ bíi gílóòbù alogíìnì.

> [The hunter told us that the eyes of this spirit . . . Oh! Do you know the extra headlight sometimes affixed to the motor vehicle to improve illumination? He said each of the eyes was as big as that. He said each of them shone equally as bright, like the halogen bulb.][7]

If Akíntáyò's description of the eyes here is not disingenuous but rather a creative reconstruction, the discrepancy between a particular detail in both halves of the narrative of Ràsákì Àlàó Adúpé, first performed by the presenter and then by the hunter, is more definite.[8] Both feature a description of a fit of cold and immobility that the hunter suffers upon his encounter with the antagonist civet. Akíntáyò's narration situates this occurrence in the moment immediately after the wounded civet is dealt the machete's blow. In Adúpẹ̀'s version, however, the hunter is hit at the point when the animal is being gutted. Similarly, in the presenter's version of the Ògúndélé Alájáníbọn Dẹ́tunhà, 'àhàyá bíi mẹ́rin àbí márùn-ún' [about four or five pellets] fall from the antagonist's chest after the Ògún ritual. Dẹ́tunhà later says there are more than 15 pellets.[9] In the solo performance of the narrative on the 13 February 2005 edition of the programme, Akíntáyò says that the àjé antagonist dies. The 20 February 2005 edition was intended to correct the goof. The antagonist, according to Dẹ́tunhà himself, survives and still lives.

The radio, perhaps the cheapest means of access to broadcasting in the world, sometimes mimics conversation. It is in order to simulate the conversational feel that the narrator sometimes assumes that s/he is addressing listeners who are physically present. Listening to a narrative in such natural contexts as a church hall or a local pub, the listener may take for granted the significance of extra-verbal signs, like gestures, facial kinemes, and even silences. Such seemingly secondary factors, like age, height and appearance, of not only the performer but also the audience, might also be crucial to the eventual process of meaning-making. The radio, however, is blind. It relies entirely on the auditory channel to invoke its message. Lewis (1981:9) quite interestingly considers this handicap a merit, and, in a manner of speaking, he sees the radio as a 'visual medium':

> To say that radio is a visual medium when in one sense it is completely non-visual is to bring out the way in which radio encourages the listener's imagination to visualize what he is listening to, to create for himself the visual dimension he is apparently deprived of, to construct the setting and appearance of the characters from the clues that words and sounds provide.

Lewis' point is significant in its observation of the radio audience as having a higher and more independent responsibility as co-mythmakers than an audience that is physically present. Nevertheless, Lewis's statements downplay the significance of the performer's physical presence with the audience, a facility that the radio does not guarantee. On *Ọdẹ Akọni*, the guest narrators, who are used to the natural physical context of conversation and not educated in the electronic media translation of physical signs, sometimes mar their own efforts at signification. In his broadcast narrative, Moses Adébóyè Ògúnwálé illustrates the height of his spirit captor by comparing it to that of the host.[10] He says that even as short as the latter is, he is towering compared to the spirits. Though the audience gets the hint that the spirit characters are indeed very short, the medium has denied them visual access to the simile invoked to stress it. In his description of the mysterious misanthrope of Ìkẹ̀rẹ̀ Forest, Múdàsírù Ọdẹ́wùmí Òjó of Ìméléke village, near Oyo, says: '*Ibi apá báyìí, awọ ẹtu ni . . . Ìhààyín, awọ ìgalà ni. Ẹ̀wù t'ọ́ wọ̀ báyìí, awọ akítì ni*, àt'erí i rẹ̀' [This side of him was a duiker's skin . . . This part, a deer's skin. His dress was made of the hide of baboon, with its head]. Even if the audience visualises the character's skin and the dress of baboon's hide, nothing in the description or the entire narrative text suggests the particular part of the character's body identified as '*ibi apá báyìí*' [this side] or '*ìhààyín*' [this part]. Similarly, narrators not only claim to have trophies of their encounters with the mysterious Other, but sometimes display them. This exhibitionist temper is appropriately illustrated in Rábíù Òjó's adornment of his *egúngún* costume with the skin of the mysterious civet cited earlier. Accordingly, many hunters display the memorabilia of their encounters in the radio studios, with the host attempting to describe them to the audience (see Plates 3.1 and 3.2). In these cases, the listener's only choice is to 'visualize' (Lewis 1981), sometimes at a distant remove from the narrator's fictive intention.

As early as 1932, barely two decades after radio became institutionally established as a medium of broadcast, the German dramatist, Brecht (1993), called attention to the handicap of the radio as a one-way medium of communication. He considers the radio broadcast as a form of tyranny through monologue because it proscribes the listener from 'talking back'. Brecht ultimately identifies the need to create 'an ear' for the radio to facilitate a robust intercourse between it and the listener as a way to humanise both parties. The audience of such narrative as *Ọdẹ Akọni*, designed to mimic human conversation, is always an active one to such an extent that it becomes a partner in the performance. *Ọdẹ Akọni*, a programme intended for an audience of hundreds of thousands, resolves the problem of audience participation in two major ways: namely, by putting the host in the role of a proxy audience whenever the hunter-protagonist himself is performing, and by providing an opportunity for listeners to call in at the end of the programme. As a solo listener, however, Akíntáyọ̀ does not in any way represent the performative potential of that multitude of listeners. The radio performance, in this aspect, merely aspires to the kind of performative arena it cannot afford.

The call-in period is designed to empower the audience to participate. Its unavoidable placement at the end of the main performance, however, diminishes its performative immediacy. Unlike the host, who can play the role of immediate audience and interlocutor, the telephone does not allow the remote audience to access such adjunct performative roles as questioning and prompting the narrator, and thereby contributing to the ultimate shape of the narrative text. Moreover, it is important to note that many members of the radio audience might not be able to afford the cost of telephoning; others who attempt to call never get through. Even some of the calls that do get through to the studios sometimes either fail midway or are utterly inaudible. Shingler and Wieringa (1998) usefully remind us of the magnitude of the host's power to determine which caller has access to the microphone. The host and/or the producer have the power to determine when the calls start to come in, when they stop, or whether they are to be entertained at all.

The hunter's narrative as a radio performance is a commodified item; as such, the presenter is mindful of the length of story allowed in each session. In the natural conversational form that the radio performance imitates, narratives ensue as a matter of course with the performers telling their stories spontaneously at opportune moments during the interlocution. The radio narratives, however, come in bits, punctuated by advertisements. The cost of seeking out hunters from remote villages, persuading them to come and tell their stories on air, providing them with lodging, and paying them honoraria seems to have inscribed a high value on each of the hunter's narratives. Narrative performance as an exercise in reliving an event in a different time and space is amenable to some sort of abridgment or fleshing out in accordance with the performer's whim and goal. Conversational narratives of relatively enduring length are often sustained by description and proliferating sub-plots that effectively enhance the suspense. But even in such a context, the narrator can be seen as ambling resolutely home to the final core of the story. In the radio performance of the hunters' narratives, however, the presenter's insistence on stretching the story over the one-and-a-half-hour session becomes so overt that the listener sometimes becomes exasperated. The host's elaborate repetition of the details given earlier in the narrative before the last advertisement break is a recurrent example. Báyọ̀ Adébọ̀wálé, the flutist, also subtly abets the presenter in his attempt to fill the time. In his occasional interjection with the flute, the host sometimes commits more time than necessary to the ensuing mock quarrel between them. Though the exchange is mostly very rich in humour, a concentration of it, designed to pad out the narrative session, is cloying and detracts from listening pleasure. The rationing of the story as an item of value is best illustrated in the performance of Améringùn.[11] The vivacious old hunter simply wants to go on naturally to narrate the story behind his name 'He-who-mounts-the-elephant'. The presenter cautions him that the story is better preserved for another edition. The old man, hitherto defiant of the presenter's moderation, agrees to save the story for another day. Perhaps the honorarium is worth a second trip.

Commerce creeps into the framing of the show, as well. Advertisements appear not only during breaks in the narrative, but also at the beginning and the end of the programme. Consider, for example, the following stunt, which creeps stealthily in with the opening 'Ẹ káalẹ́ o. Ẹ kú ìgbádùn ètò Ọdẹ Akọni' [Good evening, I wish you a happy listening to Ọdẹ Akọni narrative], represents one such attempt not only to share the arena of performance with the hunter but to exploit the hunting profession as a sort of qualification:

> Ọ̀dọ̀ àgbàlágbángbá ọdẹè kan l'à n lọ. Ámbàlí Ọdẹ l'ògbólógbòó ọdẹ yìí n jẹ́. Ó j'ogún iṣẹ́ ọdẹ l'ọ́dọ̀ ọ bàbá a rè ni. Òhun náà ti k'ojú ẹran abìjà rí. Ọ̀pọ̀lọpọ̀ iwin nínúu 'gbó ni wọ́n ti jọ gbé pẹ́régi ka'ná. Irú ọdẹ yìí wúlò f'ọmọ Nàìjíríà. Lọ́nà wo? Rí Ámbàlí Ọdẹ fún gbogbo àrùnkarùn tí n yọ ó lénu lágọ̀ọ́ ara à rẹ, àti pé gbogbo aláwàáàrí ọ y'ojú sí wọn . . . Ámbàlí Ọdẹ n bẹ ní Agboolé e Gbárayílẹ̀ l'Ókè Adú n'Bàdàn.

> [I tell you about a certain old and experienced hunter. This valiant hunter is called Ámbàlí the Hunter. He inherited hunting from his very father. He himself has confronted many ferocious animals. He has done battle with many spirits of the forest. In what way is this hunter beneficial to the people of Nigeria? See Ámbàlí the Hunter for cure to any disease you may be suffering from. Also, all those who have failed in one undertaking or the other could also consult him . . . Ámbàlí the Hunter is based in Gbárayílẹ̀ Compound, Ókè Adú, Ibadan.][12]

Many such advertisements punctuate the narrative sessions. Sometimes as many as five breaks occur, intruding at crucial moments in the narrative, thereby creating a sort of forced suspense, created not through artistic building of tension but through the abrupt suspension of narrative performance. In the instance cited above, the advertisement intrudes so rudely, and without any preliminary apology, that the listener is first stunned by the sudden rupture in the narrative symmetry. S/he realises only some seconds later that the intrusion is an advertisement stunt.

The broadcast media have exposed the Yoruba hunter. This exposure comes with a dual implication: it entrenches the primordial identity of the hunter as a member of an elite corps, while, at the same time, shattering the idea of secrecy that has, for a long time, reinforced that elitist identity.

Notes

1. *Ọdẹ Akọni*, 28/09/2003.

2. *Ọdẹ̀tẹ̀dò* resumed on BCOS on 13 March 2008, but by the beginning of 2010, it was taken off the air again.

3. Head of hunters.

4. *Ọdẹ Akọni*, 24/12/2006.

5. Ràsákì Àlàó Adúpẹ́, *Ọdẹ Akọni*, 26/06/2005.

6. *Ọdẹ Akọni*, 12/09/2004.

7. *Ọdẹ Akọni*, 12/09/2004.

8. *Ọdẹ Akọni*, 26/06/2005.

9. *Ọdẹ Akọni*, 20/02/2005.

10. *Ọdẹ Akọni*, 10/12/2006.

11. *Ọdẹ Akọni*, 12/09/2004.

12. *Ọdẹ Akọni*, 10/12/2006.

CONCLUSION

In writing this book I set out with an essentially tripartite focus. The first objective was to show that art is not limited to the easily recognisable forms. Narration, one of the most fluid and ubiquitous of arts, is examined in the light of this. The Yoruba hunters' culture is an especially suitable case study because it putatively taboos narrativity. An ample view of the Yoruba worldviews is accessible through the hunter's eye; as the second objective, I therefore attempted to use the hunters' narratives as an index to understanding some aspects of this worldview. The ultimate intention was to add to the existing definitions the Yoruba worldview. For the third objective, I examined performance as an exercise in mediating the dialectics of tradition and change, Selfness and Otherness, and art and life.

The dynamic nature of both Yoruba culture generally and the hunters' culture in particular has made it intractable to a permanent definition. Existing studies on the Yoruba hunters' culture therefore are not exhaustive. In their attempts to describe the nature and the process of the performative aspects of the culture, these studies overlook the performer's creative propensity for breaching norms, a feat to which the Yoruba hunter is naturally predisposed. Secondly, these studies do not typically consider the complexity and eclecticism of the composition of the hunter's person and art. Modern literary narratives have also employed the hunter's persona and/ or his description of reality. It is in the sober realisation of the status of man as a partner, not the sole factor, in the determination of earthly matters that these works have mostly appropriated the hunter's vision. Apart from a body of folktales in a section of Herskovits and Herskovits' (1958) *Dahomean narrative: A cross-cultural analysis*, no known work has attempted to collect and study the hunters' narratives as an alternative understanding of the universe.

In the broader area of African literary and cultural discourse, most of the existing analytic and theoretical models have not been entirely appropriate in explicating African cultural forms. One example is the presentation of stories as inherited articles, set in stone, and passed down from previous generations. Such an approach overlooks the performative imperative that imbues narrative with so much modification and, in fact, deviation that the ensuing product becomes a different work of art in its own right.

Closely related is a tendency to overlook the extent of interweaving of life and narrative art. The reigning understanding that the fabulous narrative mirrors life is only partly true as far as the hunter is concerned; for him, the 'fabulous' is life. In his world, the reality-fable borderline thins out until it is hardly visible. This is exactly where the contextualist counsel to consider the sociological aspects of performance is important. In the appraisal of the hunters' narratives, a sole dependence on text might result in a taxonomy that brackets outright fiction with narrative recollection. The dualist interpretation holds sway over many descriptions of African cultural forms. Sharp dividing lines are put between such poles as good and evil, spirit and matter, and the real and the fabulous without due consideration for the intersection and impermanence that characterise them. This formation is entrenched by the wholesale employment of the Western interpretive tools in the readings of such cultural sites.

Existing literary and cultural theories provide useful insights, but none is exclusively appropriate as an interpretive tool in approaching the hunters' narratives. Structuralism, for example, is an elegant and neat analytic method, especially where the motifs of conflict and opposition are overt and the morphological comparison of one narrative with another is necessary. Structuralism does not, however, anticipate a situation in which the opposition is either secondary or invisible. Even as its later outgrowth, narratology, seeks attention for such marginal expressive forms as conversation and military parade, its prescription excludes the consideration of specific contextual instances of performance as a way of determining performative licence. The scientificity of structuralism also, in a way, abets the kind of objectivist and positivist attitude that portrays the alternative reality of certain narratives as alogical and therefore inferior to modern Western realism (Drewal 1991; Rabkin 1977).

It is in the consideration of the individual performative instances that novelty is discovered. Bakhtin (1981) sets off the influential theoretical trend that demands sympathetic and attentive consideration for every cultural and ideological expression. Dialogism, Bakhtin's term for this liberalised space, supposes that a language breathes and lives because it relates with another. Thus, opposite positions such as the Self and the Other, spirit and matter, and the real and the fabulous not only relate to but, more significantly, influence each other. The poststructuralist cultural theories contemporaneous with Bakhtin further examine the idea of exactitude and permanence in relation to various ideological and cultural constructs. Gates Jr (1983) traces the origin of semantic uncertainty to many precolonial African forms; Bhabha (1994) particularly argues that the existence of interstitial spaces such as diaspora, mulatto and cosmopolis supplants such oppositions as coloniser/colonised, indigenous/exotic, and so on. Their overplay of the idea of impermanence notwithstanding, these poststructuralist thoughts give insight to the preponderance of the intersection of different cultural spaces, thereby reviewing the formation of cultural difference and originary.

In the book I partly adopt the poststructuralist supposition that praxis demotes what codes often seem to immediately suggest. As such, the hunter's story that is not told is told. The narrative breach of this ethic of silence did not start with the intervention of broadcast media but has rather been a primordial part of the culture. Even in Yoruba culture, where the hunter puts a premium on taciturnity, he nevertheless tells his stories. The emergence of the radio as a medium of narrative performance highlights this silence-narrativity double-bind. It reveals the dynamics of the institution of norms, creative breaches of those norms, and the eventual popular reception of that breach. The factors at play are partly bound up with contemporary socio-economic needs. In traditional Yoruba society, there were such needs as initiating the youth into the hunters' guild and thereby making him a potential warrior, endearing the hunter's merchandise to the prospective customers, and maintaining a good hunter-non-hunter relation. The unbridled narrativisation of the hunter's experience jeopardises all of these roles. Today, as in the past, most of these needs persist but have been subordinated by more formidable contemporary ones. They include the need to give cultural expressions and identities prominence as global cultural production becomes more competitive, and the sublime but more determinant economic need.

The analysis of the narrative performances confirms the hunter as a representation of man's attempt to pacify and domesticate the unknown and the feared. As the hunter represents the success of man in this attempt, he at once represents man's failure to dominate the same. The corollary definition of the world is therefore a space where actors – human, animal, spirit and vegetal – contend eternally. None is assured final and continuous domination over the others. Another emergent possibility is symbiosis. Situations inaugurated by conflict do not necessarily resolve through clear victory and defeat. The Yoruba world accommodates the resolution of even mortal opposition into a beneficial alliance. As such, the àjẹ́, the spirit, the animal and the tree emit the type of energy – whether malignant or benevolent – required by their relationship with man. But the preponderance of conflict does not necessarily make the forest – the Other half of the Yoruba world – an absolute conflict zone where man either triumphs, perishes or seeks diplomatic resolution. As in the human world, the infinitude of the forest surpasses total narrative understanding. Conflict might either be aborted or never begin at all.

The hunter-narrator can only be said to have deviated from the norm by half. Since he sometimes sees the narrative performance as part of a continuum with tradition, he also thinks himself a custodian of that tradition. As Bhabha (1994) repeatedly notes, performativity supplants the concept of originary. All cultures breathe and thrive not only in renewal, but also in the adoption of contemporary idioms. The claim that a particular form is traditional therefore comes with some qualification. A close reading of some Yoruba forms that are considered traditional, even in the orthodox sense, reveals the presence of exotic elements. For example, Òtúá Méjì, an *odù* of *Ifá* – a divination system considered by Yoruba to be of primordial origin – is a narrative of the origin of Islam (Abimbola 1969a). Considering that *Ifá* practice is not only considered inviolably closed to the infusion of new elements but also of pre-Islamic origin (Abimbola 1976), this narrative attests to a predisposition of the Yoruba culture to new elements that advance it. Such exotic elements are not in this sense, seen as importation as such, but are rather part of the permissible regeneration that began when the cultural form inaugurated itself. The growing popularity of the performance of hunters' narratives on air, even among those who initially opposed it, becomes understandable in this sense.

The example of the performance of hunters' narratives is proof that art is not limited to identifiable normative forms. What is identified in the book as hunters' narratives is so dependent on informal communication that it has no definite name in Yoruba. Yet, as shown in the analysis, the deployment of such figural devices as proverb, metaphor, *ọfọ̀* and *oríkì*, as well as the descriptive evocation of characters and events, attest to its artistry. The popular audience it commands as a radio series is an additional proof. The performer therefore is not just the narrator of the *àlọ́*, the *ìjálá* poet or the *alárìnjó* dramatist. The bus driver who recounts his encounter with the traffic warden might equally be a performer. The quality and success of individual performative efforts vary, but many are so pleasing that the performers are asked to tell the story again some other time.

Cultural change may immediately survive the tremor that attends that change, but such change sometimes comes with its own set of limitations. There is, for example, the popular view that writing as a medium of narration falls short of the performative fullness of the orality it aspires to represent. A related view supposes that written and oral narratives, however much one presumes to have adopted from the other, are two entirely different media. To see writing as a modern outgrowth of the oral narrative, in this view, is to downplay the equal currency and continuation of orality as an entirely different and peculiar medium of narration. There is an interesting parallel of this situation in the emergence of radio as a medium of narration. Even as radio narration does not differ as much from its parent, informal spoken communication, as does writing, it nevertheless presents its own limitations. Radio hides certain aspects of performance and performances must fit within the economic strictures of the programme.

The performance of hunters' narratives examined here reveals the presence of art in a performative space that is not nominally identified as art. The corollary recommendation is that literary, cultural and performance studies need to focus more intently on related cultural sites in order to reflect more accurately on the manner in which routine human communication not only influences art, but also becomes one. Instances of such performativity abound and emerge every day in such forms as religious sermons, radio chit-chat programmes, television reality shows, and disc jockeys' (DJs) creative selection and reworking of musical records to retain the attention of an audience at a party.

There are many canonical studies on specific African performance cultures. Many of these – some now dating from half a century ago – have attempted commendable descriptions of the different forms they set out to examine. But as thorough and circumspect as these accounts have been, the contemporary exigencies that continuously redefine performance have made many aspects of such studies worthy of review. For example, Babalola's (1966) work on *ìjálá* does not anticipate the breach of tradition introduced in the refrain songs in Alabi Ogundepo's art (Adeduntan 2003). The poetics of *ìyèrè* described by Olatunji (1984) and Abimbola (1976) is supplanted by the example of Ifáyẹmí Ẹlẹ́buìbọn, who freely uses the form as a medium of social commentary. The very recent example of an *èsà* poet, Àsàbí Ọ̀jẹ̀ Afẹ́nápa, who extensively uses songs from other forms like *ìjálá* and Sàngó worship songs, also invites a review of Olajubu's (1970) description of *iwì egúngún*.[1] It is therefore recommended that rather than see such performative divergences as 'rogue' types that violate tradition, scholars should devote their efforts to studying and understanding them.

Notes

1.   Performance of poetry of the *egúngún*.

Appendix A

The narrative of Músílíù Àlàgbé Fìríàáríkú[1]

Fìríàáríkú: Ní ojó tí mọ lọ dẹ Igbó Oníwòrò, mo rí nkan ìyanu. Bí ọ̀ bá jé pé mo múra ló'ọ́ látinúu'lé pé n'torí aìímọ̀, áàh! eégún ọdẹ ọ̀ bá fẹ́ẹ̀ gbé ọ̀jẹ́ n'jọ́ náà o. Ọ́ dàbí nkan.

Mo ti n dẹgbẹ́ bọ̀ látàárọ̀. Mọ bá ìyá yìí ní nkan bí aago wẹ́wàá. Èmi 'ò sì d'ẹgbó yìí rí. Sùgbọ́n n'gbà mo bá a, mo rí i l'ọ̀ọ́kán, ọ́ gbálẹ̀ ẹ'bẹ̀, ó jókòó n'ídìí igi

'Ẹ nlẹ́ o, màmá. Ẹ nlẹ́ o, màmá.' Kọ̀ dáhùn.

'Ọ́ dáa, t'ọ̀ọ́ bá dáhùn, ọ̀ọ́ dáhùn náà nù-un. Èmi n bá tèmi í lọ.'

Adédùntán: Ẹẹ̀ sì lè padà?

Fìríàáríkú: T'éèyàn bá padà bẹ́ẹ̀, kọ̀ dáa. Eléyùùun 'ẹé s'ọdẹ nù-un. Mọ bá n lọ. Mọ kọjá a rẹ̀ tán, mo ní n ọ́ já ọ̀nà kan, ọ̀dọ̀ ìyá yìí n'mo tún já.

'Haà! Èéti jé? Ẹ ha pọ̀ n'nú u'gbó yìí bẹ́ẹ̀ ni?' Mọ bá tún gba ọ̀nà mìì. Mo tún lọ, ọ̀dọ̀ ìyá yìí náà n'mo tún já sí. Mọ wáá rò ó: kíni mọ fẹ́ẹ́ se báyìí o. Mọ wá t'ọwọ́ b'àpò, mọ fà'bínú yọ.

Adédùntán: Ẹ t'ọwọ́ bọ gbérí?

Fìríàáríkú: Mọ t'ọwọ́ bọ'kùn, mọ fà'bínú yọ. Mo ní l'ágbára baba à mi, iró, kò ní hun mí. Mo pè é; mo pè'yá yìí. Kọ̀ dáhùn. Mọ lọ́ dáa. Odò kan sì nbẹ nítòsí ibẹ̀, mọ bá gba ẹ̀gbẹ́ odò hun lọ, mọ dá odò hun kọjá . . .

Adédùntán: L'ẹ́hìn ìgbà tẹ́ẹ ti sàà'gùn tán?

Fìríàáríkú: Hin. Mọ dá odò hun kọjá tí mo sì mọ̀ pé mo ti dá odò kọjá. Sùgbọ́n n'gbà n ó tún wo ẹ̀gbẹ́ ẹ̀ mi, àfi bí ìgbà èèyàn sùn t'ọ́ wáá ya'jú, mọ bá tún r'íyàá yìí.

'Aàh! Ọ màmà ní nkan á bá mi í se o. Èe wa ti jé?' Mọ wá rántí kíni kan tí nbẹ n'bi gbérí ì mi. Ojú ù mi wáá yà. Mo gòkè odò, mọ bá já ojú ọ̀nà kan; mọ já ojú u títì. Mo dé ìlú kan, àá pè é ní *Ògbògbò*, ní *area* ìjẹbú-Òde.

Adédùntán: Ìjẹbú-Óde lẹ ti lọ dè'gbẹ, lát'Ìpínlẹ̀ Ọ̀sun?

Fìríàáríkú: Hin Ìjẹbú-Òde ni. Mọ wá wọ'nú u '1é.

Wọ́n ní 'Kílódé l'átàárọ̀, baba ọdẹ?' Mo ní n 'ọ̀ mọ̀ pé'rú nkan báhun nbẹ ní *area* yín n'bíyìí. Mọ bá sáà k'álàyé, mo se fún ẹni t'ọ́ jé bàálé è mi.

Ó ní 'Haà! Ọlọ́'un mà yọ ọ́ o! Ìwọ l'à bá máa pè ní 'Fìríàáríkú'.'

Mo ní 'Hìín? Kí ló sẹlẹ̀?' Ó l'ọdẹ kan ọ dẹ 'gbó hun kọ́ bọ rí. Ó ní kọ̀ s'ọ́dẹ kan tí ọ́ dẹ'gbó hun tí ọ́ bọ̀.

Adédùntán: Ibi t'ẹẹ ti njẹ́ orúkọ yín t'ẹ n jẹ́ l'ónìí nù-un?

Fìríàáríkú: Ibẹ̀ gan n mo ti n jẹ́ 'Fìríàáríkú'. N náà sì ni gbogbo Ìwó mọ̀ mí sí, títí tée dé Ọláolúwa. B'ẹ́èyàn bá béèrè Músílíù tí wọn 'ọ̀ bá dáákọ Fìríàáríkú, ẹ̀ẹ̀ leè rí i.

Fìríàáríkú: The day I went to hunt in the Forest of Oníwòrò, I saw a thing of wonder. Had I not equipped myself properly from home, *the hunter's masquerade would have perished in the grove* that day. It was a wonder.

I had been hunting since morning. At about ten o' clock [in the night], I saw a woman. I had never gone to that forest before then. When I saw her, she sat down under a tree, and the place was well swept.

'Hi, woman', I greeted. 'Hi, woman.' She did not respond.

'Well, if you do not answer me, that is your problem,' I said to her. 'I am going.'

Adédùntán: You did not turn back?

Fìríàáríkú: No going back. Whoever goes back that way is not a true hunter. So I kept going, intending to link another road. However, I ended up where this woman was sitting.

'What is this,' I marvelled. 'Are you this many in this forest?' I left again, taking an entirely different route. But I again ended up where this woman sat. What is to be done now, I reflected. So, *I put hand in my pocket and brought out a fit of anger.*

Adédùntán: You put your hand in the cloak?

Fìríàáríkú: *I put hand in my gut and brought out a fit of anger.* I invoked my forefathers against any failure. I then called this woman again, but she did not answer. Now there was a river close to the place. I took a route to the river, and crossed it over.

Adédùntán: After that invocation?

Fìríàáríkú: Yes. I crossed the river and was sure I did. But when I looked up – just as if it had all been a dream – I saw this woman [before me].

'What have you with me?' I exclaimed. 'What is the matter?' Then I remembered *one thing* I had in my cloak. [I used it and] my eyes opened. I crossed the river and took a road that led me to the highway. I got to a place called Ógbógbó in Ìjẹ̀bú Òde.

Adédùntán: You mean you went to hunt in Ìjẹ̀bú Òde? From Osun State?

Fìríàáríkú: Yes, it was Ìjẹ̀bú Òde. So, I went into the house.

'Oh hunter, where have you been all this while?' [the people at home asked]. I told them that I did not know that such a thing exists in the forests there. I reported everything to my host.

'Oh, that was really a close one,' he said. '"Fìríàáríkú" [At-close-quarters-with-death] would be an appropriate name for you.'

'Why? What is the matter?' I queried. He said no hunter ever went into that forest and came back. None had ever.

Adédùntán: That was how you got that name?

Fìríàáríkú: That was how I became Fìríàáríkú. That is the name all the people of Ìwó call me, even up to Olá Olúwa. If you identify me as Musiliu without adding Fìríàáríkú, you might not be able to get to me.

Appendix B

The narrative of Rábíù Òjó[2]

Òjó: T'áa bá tí r'íbi ọlọ́gẹ̀dẹ̀ gbé n su, wọn ọ́ wàá mú'míi rẹ̀, wọn ó fi í ínú agolo. Eléyùùn, mọ gbọ́njú bá a ni, nítorí èdọ̀ ẹran ni mọ jẹ dàgbà. Aá wàá lọ ọ'bí tí n yàgbẹ́ sí hun, ẹnìkan ó dú'ó nbẹ̀. Aá ti 'á sọ pé k'ọ́mọ̀ọ̀kan ọ́ bá ni gbé kinní hun ka'ná.

Adédùntán: Imí hun?

Òjó: Imí hun.

Adédùntán: Ẹ ti bu nkan míì sí i o.

Òjó: Aà bu nkan míì si i. T'ọ́ bá di p'ó hó kọ̀tọ̀kọ̀tọ̀, ẹran hun ó kú'ò n'bi ọ wà, yíó lọ ọ'bí tí í gbe é yàgbẹ́. T'ọ́ bá ti dé orí ibi t'ó gbéé yàgbẹ́ hun, aà gbọdọ̀ yìnbọn sí i l'órí ẹ̀. Àmọ́ tí 'ọ̀ bá tíì dé'bẹ̀ t'áa bá e yìnbọn sí i, aá pa á. Àmọ́ t'ọ́ bá wà l'órí i kiní hun, t'eèyàn bá yìnbọn sí i, èèyàn 'ò níí pa á. Eléyìí wáá gun orí awà, ó n yàgbẹ́ . . .

Adédùntán: Èwo ní n j'áwà?

Òjó: Ibi tí wọn maá yàgbẹ́ sí hun ni. Ọ́ n yàgbẹ́. Nígbàt'ó kú'ò, njé yíó maa lọ la pè é. A gbé 'bọn lé e. N'gbà a dé bẹ:

'Irun l'ó kó yìí! Ọmú rèé! Ọlọ́gẹ̀dẹ̀ la yínbọn sí, élèyíì ti jẹ́?' Ọmú n se langalanga.

Adédùntán: Ẹ bá'run dídì l'órí ẹ̀?

Òjó: Irun dídì nbẹ l'órí. Ibi ìdí n'sàlẹ̀, ọlọ́gẹ̀dẹ̀ ni. Irun nbẹ n'bẹ̀ papàá.

'Báwo laá ti s'eléyìí báyìí? Eléyìí 'ò seé gbé lọọ'lé.' Mọ bá lọ ké sí bàbá kan t'ó jẹ Ọlọ́ọ́dẹ n'gbà náà – bàbá a t'èmi ti kúrò lórí àléfà ọdẹ n'gbà náà. Mọ bá lọ rèé fi hàn á. Ó ní a máa rí bẹ́ẹ̀. Ó ní s'émi 'ọ̀ mọ pé ọ́ pọ̀ n'nú èèyàn t'ó se pé ẹranko ni. N'gbàtí a wáá rí i báhun, tí a gbé e dé'lé, a ké e é méjì. Kọ́dà, awọ ọ rẹ̀ papàá n bẹ l'ára eégún ù mi.

Adédùntán: Abalaa'bi èèyàn rẹ̀ nkọ́? Ṣ'ẹ́ẹ b'óhun náà ni?

Òjó: Abalaa'bi èèyàn rẹ̀ kò ní bíbó mọ́, nígbà tó se pé a gé e ni.

Adédùntán: N'gbà ẹ gé e méjì, abala t'èèyan nkọ́? Báwo lẹ ṣe ṣe é?

Òjó: Mo gbé é kalẹ̀ s'ọ́dọ̀ Bàbá Ọdẹ ìgbà náà. Ó ní ẹran ni?

Adédùntán: Báwo ni wọ́n ṣe ṣe é?

Òjó: Wọ́n gé e kéékèèké, wọ́n há a f'áwọn obìnrin.

Adédùntán:	Wọ́n há a?
Òjó:	Sùgbọ́n wọ́n ti fá ọmú u rẹ̀ kú'ò n'bẹ̀. Gbogbo ohun tí n jẹ́ orí hun gangan alára, wọ́n kó o kúrò n'bẹ̀.
Adédùntán:	Orí tó d'irun?
Òjó:	Gbogbo 'ẹ̀ ni wọ́n kó kú'ò n'bẹ̀. Wọ́n ní ẹran ọlọ́gẹ̀dẹ̀ ni; wọ́n ní kèé s'èèyàn. Wọ́n ní gbogbo ẹranko t'ọ́ wà n'gbó náà ní í maá d'èèyàn á wá'lé l'álẹ́.
Òjó:	Wherever we saw the droppings of a civet, we always put such droppings inside a can. I grew up knowing this [magical ritual]. I was brought up on a diet of animals' liver, you know. Now someone would then wait and keep watch on that spot where the civet had defecated, while another puts the can on fire.
Adédùntán:	That can of civet's droppings?
Òjó:	Yes, the droppings.
Adédùntán:	Would you add anything?
Òjó:	No, we would not. The moment the content started to boil, the animal would leave its present position and head for its usual place of defecation. The animal must not be fired at right at the place. If we did, we would miss. But if we aimed at it before it got to the place, we would hit it. You always miss a defecating civet. Now this very civet is seated on *awà* . . .
Adédùntán:	What is *awà*?
Òjó:	That is the place where the civets defecate. This very civet was defecating. As it made to go, I fired a shot at it. When we got to the place where it fell, we saw the civet cat in braids, and with human breasts too! Wonder! The breasts dangled like human breasts!
Adédùntán:	You saw braids on its head?
Òjó:	Yes, the head was braided. But the lower part was a civet. Complete with tail and all.
	'What are we going to do with it?' We asked ourselves in confusion. 'We must not take it home.' So I took it to the man who was the head of hunters of the time, for my father had passed on at the time – his name was Laani. I took it to him. He explained that such thing was usual as there are creatures that double as animal and human. So, we cut the animal into two. The skin now adorns the costume of my egúngún.
Adédùntán:	What about the human half? Did you skin it too?
Òjó:	No we cut it off.

Adédùntán: After cutting it off, what became of the human half?

Òjó: I left it with the Baba Ọdẹ [Ọlọ́ọ́dẹ] of the time. He said it was edible.

Adédùntán: What did he do with it?

Òjó: He cut it up and shared the meat among the women.

Adédùntán: Shared it?

Òjó: But he had cut away the breasts and the head.

Adédùntán: The head with the braids?

Òjó: Yes. He had scraped off the braids. He said it was no more human but a civet. He said many animals in the forest often do change into human form in order to come to town anyway.

Appendix C

The narrative of Jóògún Àlàdé[3]

Jóògún: Ojó kẹn, èmi yìí nẹ́ẹ̀, b'émi ti mọ kékeé yìí nẹ́ẹ̀ ni . . . Òjò àkọ́rọ tíí kọ́ọ́ rọ̀ nì, ẹ mọ̀ pé omi mọọ́ wọ́n nínọ́ọ'jù.

Adédùntán: Bẹ́ẹ̀ ni.

Jóògún: Mọ wáá dúró níbi ihò àpáta à kẹn. Mo ní túláàsì, àwọn ẹrẹn ọ́ maa wá mọ omi níhìín. Ìgbà tọ́ pẹ́, mọ bá rí [èèyàn] bí àwọn Fílànì, ọ́ jẹ́ mẹ́ta.

Adédùntán: Fílànì mẹ́ta?

Jóògún: Obì'in ni wọ́n o. Wọ́n wá pọn'mi l'ódò ni. Bí èèyàn ni wọ́n wá pọn'mi. Mọ sáà dákẹ́; ǹń sáà n wò wọ́n. Wọn ò rí mi o. Bí wọn se pọn'mi tẹ́n – èyìn igi nlá kẹn wáá n bẹ – wọ́n bọ́ s'ẹ́yìn igi nì, n ò rí wọn mọ́. Mọ sáà dákẹ́ títítítí. Toò, ìgbà tọ́ pẹ́, tí n wo ẹ̀yìn igi nì, ìgalà ni mo rí tí wọ́n tẹ̀lé'raa wọn.

Adédùntán: Ibi ẹ̀yìn igi tí àwọn Fúlànì yẹn kó sí?

Jóògún: Ibi ẹ̀yìn igi tí àwọn kiní yẹn pọnmi lọ ni. Àwọn ìgalà. Wọ́n tẹ̀lé'raa wọn; mẹ́ta

Adédùntán: Ìgalà mẹ́ta náà ni? Fúlànì obìnrín mẹ́ta náà ló dẹ̀ lọọ'bẹ̀?

Jóògún: Hẹn. Àwọn mẹ́ta náà ni. Ìgbàa wọ́n dé, mọ bá yìnbọn s'íkẹn n'bẹ̀. Ọ̀kẹ́n tí mo yìbọn sí nì, tíẹ̀ é bá se pé àwọn bàbá bá wa lọọ'gbẹ́ ni, aà lè kun ú.

Òjó: Kílódé?

Jóògún: Hun t'aà fi lè kun ú ni pé ìgbà t'ẹ́rẹn ẹ̀ yẹn subú lu'lẹ̀, ègbẹ́ kẹn ẹrẹn, ègbẹ́ kẹn èèyẹ̀n.

Òjó: Haà!

Jóògún: Mo dé'bẹ̀ báyìí, mọ p'ẹ̀yìndà. Mọ bá họ, ó di bùdó. N'gbà mo dé bùdó, mo ní.

'Bàbá.'

Ó ní 'Hìín.'

'Mọ mà rí nkẹn.'

O ní 'Kílódé?' Mọ bá k'álàyé é 'lẹ̀ bí mo se se lákọọ́kọ́ nì. Ọ́ bá ní n mọọ n'só n'bẹ̀. N'gbà t'áa d'ọ̀ọ̀hún nìínì, ọ́ bá ní

'Araa 'hun tí àá mọ́ọ́ wí nìinì. Ọmọ kékeé kẹn ò sí mọ́'. Ọ́ bá mú aájò kẹn.

'Hẹn. Ẹ paradà. Báa bá wọ 'nú eégún, à pahúndá ni.' Ọ́ bá di ẹrẹn.

Adédùntán:	Ó di ara ẹran padà b'ó ṣe yẹ k'ó rí?
Jọ̀ọgún:	Ó di ara ẹrẹn padà. A kun ú. Sùgbọ́n Baba ọ̀ jẹ́ kí á jẹ n'bẹ̀. N'gbà a gbé ẹran nì dé'lé, a fi tọrẹ ni.

Jọ̀ọgún:	One day, my humble self, as little as I am . . . You know that water is always scarce in the forest during the first rain.
Adédùntán:	Yes.
Jọ̀ọgún:	I then kept a watch by the tunnel in a rock. I knew animals would surely come to drink at the river nearby. After a time I saw some [people] who looked like the Fulani; they were three in number.
Adédùntán:	Three Fulani?
Jọ̀ọgún:	They were women. They came to fetch water. They came in human form. I kept quiet and remained still, watching them. They did not see me. After fetching the water – there was a big tree nearby, you know – they went behind that tree and I did not see them anymore. I was quiet and still. After a long time, I saw deer file out from behind the tree.
Adédùntán:	From behind the tree where the Fulani women disappeared?
Jọ̀ọgún:	From behind the tree where those 'things' took the water to. The deer came out in a file; three of them.
Adédùntán:	The deer were three? And the Fulani women were also three in number?
Jọ̀ọgún:	Yes, they were three. When they drew near, I fired at one of them. That one I shot at, if not that our father had been with us in that expedition, we would not have been bold enough to cut it.
Òjó:	Why?
Jọ̀ọgún:	The reason is that when the animal fell, one side of it was animal, the other was human skin.
Òjó:	Ho!
Jọ̀ọgún:	When I got to the spot, I fled in horror. I ran back to base. When I got there, I said:
	'Father.'
	'Yes,' he answered.

'I saw something strange' [I told him].

'What is it?' he asked. So I told him all. He asked me to take him there. When we got to the place, he told me:

'This is a validation of what I always tell you that none of you is a little child anymore.' So he took out a charm [and chanted *ọfọ̀*].

'Now transform, for *when a man puts on the egúngún costume, his voice changes*.' Then, it turned back to an animal.

Adédùntán: You mean the flesh became normal as if it were a wholesome deer?

Yes, it became a normal deer. We cut it up. But Father did not allow us to eat of it. Neither father nor any of us ate of it. At home, we shared it out to people.

Appendix D

The narrative of Ògúnkúnlé Òjó[4]

Ógùnkúnlé: N'jọ́ kan, ọgá à mi Ògúnọ̀ṣun ń kó wa lọọ̀'gbẹ́, èmi àt'èkejì mi Ògúnkọ́nlé. N lọ́ bá ní s'áa lè maa ǹsó d'òhun. Mo ní mọ *ready*.

'Ògúnkọ́nlé, ìwọ tẹ̀lé n' léyìn; t'ílẹ̀ bá la'ná, ìwọ sáà dì mọ́ aṣọ ọ̀ mi.'

Ìgbà t'Ọlọ́un ó seé, a bá àwọn ẹran [ẹfọ́ń]. Ìgbà t'áa bá wọn, mo gbé'bọn, mo yìnbọn sí i 'Gbìnràà!' Kí n sá ma bá a lọ lópẹ̀ẹ́títí, ẹran wó. Ìgbà t'ẹ́ran ó wòó, a ní tani ó lọ̀ pe ọgá a wa o. Mo l'émi ọ́ lọ o. Àrin ìsẹ́jú mẹ́ta náà ni nń kúkú fi d'Ágúnrege lọ́dọ̀ ọ rẹ̀.

Adédùntán: Àrin ìsẹ́jú mẹ́ta?

Ógùnkúnlé: . . . ni ń fi d'Ágúnrege lọ́dọ̀ ọ rẹ̀. Bẹ́ẹ̀ni'bi t'áa sì wí yìí tó *thirty-five miles* sí'gboro

Adédùntán: Ìsẹ́jú mẹ́ta lẹ ẹ́ sì fi rìn í?

Ógùnkúnlé: N ǹ gbọdọ̀ lò jù'sẹ́jú mẹ́ta lọ.

Adédùntán: Bàbá, òògùn lẹ fi rìn í o.

Ógùnkúnlé: Òògùn kọ́, ọgbọ́n inú àwọn ọdẹ ni. N la bá dé ọ̀dọ̀ ọgá à mi, n lọ́ bá gbé ọkọ̀ ọ rẹ̀, a bá jókòó, àt'èmi àt'ọ̀gá a wa. Ó ku bíi máìlì kan dín díẹ̀ t'aá fi dé'bẹ̀, àfi pẹ̀kí n la bá pàdé ẹran lọ́nà, èyuùun, ìyàwó. Arẹwà obìnrin ni. Ọgá a wa kí i, òhun náà k'ọ́gàá a wa. Ó kúnlẹ̀ báábáá, ó kí ọgá a wa dáadáa. N ọ̀ gbọ́ ẹwífúnmi; èmi Òjó ọdẹ ń bẹ ń'bẹ̀ ń'jọ́ náà. Ọgá a wa l'óhun ọ́ fẹ́ e, òhun náà l'óhun ọ́ fẹ́ ọ̀gá a wa.

Ó ní 'Nlọ p'óọ́ fẹ́ òhun yìí o. T'íjà bá dé o, n'jọ́ t'óọ bá p'òhun l'ọ́mọ ẹranko, n'jọ́ náà ni títán dé bá ọ ò. Ọ̀ báà nà'hun, k'óọ sá'hun l'ógbẹ́ k'éjẹ̀ ọ́ máa jáde l'ára òhun, kò s'íhun tí ọ́ sẹlẹ̀.'

Wọn bá sá fẹ́'ra a wọn lẹ́nu ù kan. Ó lóyún fún u; ó bímọ ọ̀ kínní; ó bímọ ọ̀ kejì; ó bí ọmọ ẹ̀kẹta, ìjà bá da òhun ọgá a wa pọ̀. Ìgbà t'íjà ó dèé níjọ́ náà, Ọ̀gá a wa ní 'Àb'órí ì rẹ burú ni, ìwọ ọmọ ẹranko yìí.' Ha! Iyawo l' 'Ọọ b'ọrọ jẹ lonii.' Ibi wàhálà ti dé nùun. Kí n má bá a lọ lópẹ̀ẹ́títí, ibi tí ẹranko ti kó bá ọ̀gá a wa n'ítan nùun.

Adédùntán: Ó di ẹranko?

Ógùnkúnlé: Hẹn, bẹ́ẹ̀ni.

Adédùntán: Lẹ̀sékẹsẹ̀?

Ógùnkúnlé:	Bẹ́ẹ̀ni, lẹ́sẹ̀kẹsẹ̀. N ọ̀ gbọ́ ẹwífúnmi. Lẹ́gbẹ̀ẹ́ ẹ'lé Bàbá Adémọ́lá ló ti di ẹranko l'Àgùnrege ń'bẹ̀; l'ára òkèè'Gbàdì. Ibi i wọ́n tí bẹ̀rẹ̀ síí jà nùun. Ọ̀gá a wa náà d'ọ́gbọ́n: ó d'ọ́gbọ́n-d'ọ́gbọ́n yìí, ọgbọ́n 'ò gbà. B'íyàwó se lọ ń'tiẹ̀ nùun.
Adédùntán:	Àwọn ọmọ tí obìnrin yẹn bí ńkọ́?
Ógùnkúnlé:	Àwọn ọmọ rẹ̀ mẹ́tẹ̀ẹ̀ta, ọ̀kan ti kú. Àwọn méjì t'ó kù ń bẹ. Wọ́n ń bẹ l'ọ́ọ̀dẹ̀ Ògúnọ̀sun.
Ógùnkúnlé:	One day, my master Ògúnọ̀ṣun was leading us on an expedition, I and my colleague, Ògúnkúnlé. He asked us whether we could go before him, and I told him I was ready.
	'Ògúnkúnlé,' [I called my mate], you follow me. 'If there is any danger, you just hold on to my cloth.' Luckily, we saw some animals [bufallos]. Upon sighting the animals, I aimed and fired at one, 'Bang!' To cut the story short, the animal fell. After the animal fell, I started to think about which of us would go to call our master. I volunteered to go. After all, it would take me not more than three minutes [on foot] to get to him in Agúnrege.
Adédùntán:	Not more than three minutes?
Ógùnkúnlé:	. . . to get to him in Agúnrege. And the place was about thirty-five miles to the town [Agúnrege].
Adédùntán:	And the journey would take just three minutes?
Ógùnkúnlé:	It would take me not more than three minutes.
Adédùntán:	Old one, you would use some supernatural power?
Ógùnkúnlé:	Not really. It was the wisdom of the hunters. I then got to my master. My master and I sat in his vehicle and we drove back. We were about a mile close to the place when we ran into the animal, that is the wife. She was a very beautiful woman. Our master exchanged greetings with her. She greeted our master, kneeling down in respect. This is no hearsay; I Òjó the hunter was present there that day. Our master wooed her and they both agreed to marry each other.
	She warned: 'Now that you have decided to marry me, be informed that the day you, out of anger, call me an animal, that day would be your last. It would not offend me as much if you hit me so much that I am wounded and bleeding.'
	So they got married. She became pregnant and had the first child, the second and the third child. There was a quarrel between her and

my master one day. As they quarrelled, my master angrily insulted her: 'You good-for-nothing unlucky daughter of an animal.'

'Oh!' the woman said, 'You are done for.' That was where the trouble started. To cut the long story short, that was how the animal gored our master in the thigh.

Adédùntán: She turned into an animal?

Ógùnkúnlé: Yes.

Adédùntán: Right there?

Ógùnkúnlé: Yes. It is no hearsay. She transformed into an animal by Ademọla's father's house beside Igbadi Hill. That was when the two of them started to fight. Our master tried all his power and failed. That was how the woman ran away forever

Adédùntán: What became of her children?

Ógùnkúnlé: One of the children is dead. The remaining two are still in my master's house.

Appendix E

The narrative of Ọláníyì Ọládèjọ Yáwóọrẹ́[5]

Yáwóọrẹ́: Mọ d'ẹ̀gbẹ́ lọ; ojú ù mi rí díẹ̀ ń'bẹ̀. Ìgbà tí mọ d'ẹ̀gbẹ́ lọ, mo rí ẹran yẹn, ó ń fún ọmọ l'ọmú. Ojúù mi bá bẹ̀rẹ̀ síí sú. Ìgbà t'ójú ù mí ń sú, mo ní 'Ìjọ́ tí mọ mà ti ń s'ọdẹ káàkiri, irú èyí ọ̀ mà wáyé rí. Baba à mi, ìbà rẹ lónìí o.' Mọ t'ọwọ́ bọnú u'gbèrì, mọ bẹ̀rẹ̀ sí níí f'ọwọ́ bójú pẹ̀lú egbògi kan tí *daddy* mi fún mi. Bàbá t'ó bí mi l'ọmọ ló fi isẹ́ yẹn ẹ́ lẹ̀ fún mi. Mo fi bọ́'jú, ojú ù mi là, mọ r'ẹran padà. Mọ y'ọwọ́ tì í, ìbọn ọ̀'mi sọ̀rọ̀, ẹran wó. Ìgbà tí mo dé'bẹ̀, mo ké etí i rẹ̀, mo ké ìrù u rẹ̀, mọ wá mú u wá bá àwọn tí 'an jẹ́ baba fún wa nínú ẹgbẹ́ ọdẹ pé ẹran t'áa ti ń sọ́, t'áà rí pa, ọwó ti bà á o. Sùgbọ́n nígbà t'áa padà dé'bẹ̀ ńkọ́, ìnàró l'a bá a. Àwọn t'áa sì jọ lọọ'bẹ̀ gaan, wọ́n kọ́kọ́ họ.

Yáwóọrẹ́: Mo ní 'Èé ti se? Ẹ yìnbọn fún u.' A yìnbọn, ìbọn 'ò ró. Ìgbà t'íbọn 'ò ró, mo tú ìgbàdí, mo fún u.

Adédùntán: Ẹ fi nà á?

Yáwóọrẹ́: Mo fi lù ú. Ó sì ba'lẹ̀. Ń'gbà t'ọ́ ba'lẹ̀, a kun'ran, a ru ẹran dénúu'lé, a há ẹran f'áwọn tí ọ́ j'ẹran.

Ìgbà tí a wá kan awọ ẹran sí ìta tán, mọ gba oko ọdẹ lọ. Ìgbà tí mo dé ni àwọn ọmọ wá jísẹ́ fún mi nínúu'lé wípé màmá kan wá bèèrè mi, àwọn sì sọ fún u pé n 'ò sí ń'ilé. Màmá yẹn wá padà dé ń'jọ́ kejì, ń'gbà t'áwọn ọmọ sọ fún u pé mi ì sí ń'lé.

Ó ní 'Ǹlẹ́ ọdẹ o.'

Mo ní 'Òoh, màmá.'

Ó ní 'Àwòrán a t'èyí t'óo fi se calendar sí ojúùta baba à rẹ yìí, s'óo rò pé agbára à rẹ lọ́ ká a tó báun ni? Lóòtọ́ lọ p'ẹran. A sì fún ọ pa ni. Kí ló dé t'ọọ wá n fi awọ rẹ̀ *sóò*? Kí ló dé t'ọọ wá lọ rèé kan awọ rẹ̀ mọ̀'ta gbangba? Sé ò n se gàrù nù-un pé ìwọ l'ọ p'ẹran? Sé'wọ lọ p'ẹran ni àb'aa fún ọ pa? Ọ ọ́ mọ́ pè awọ t'óo gbéé'bẹ̀hun, aṣọ tiwa lo fi nhàn fún gbogbo ayé hun?'

'Màmá, Ògún lọ́ p'ẹran.'

Ó l' 'Ògún kọ́; a yọ̀nda ẹ̀ fún ọ ni o.'

'Ìyá ẹ má bínú o. Èmi ọ̀ mọ̀ p'áṣọ yín ni o.' Ni mọ bá dọ̀bálẹ̀. Mọ wá lọ bá Olúọ́dẹ wa, Ọláifá Àdìgún, mọ sọ gbogbo ọ̀rọ̀ náà fún u. Bàbá wá sọ fún mi pé màmá yẹn ti wá l'ánàà pé òhun fẹ́ẹ́ rí mi. Ó ní kí n lọ rèé ká aṣọ ẹran. N'mọ bá fi ká a wọlé lọ.

Yáwóọrẹ́:   I went on a hunt one day. Oh, I have had my share of the [weird] encounter. While hunting, I saw the animal [deer] breastfeeding its young. Just then, I strated to feel dizzy. When I could not see properly, I was alarmed and said, 'I have never seen this type of thing all my hunting days. Oh, homage to you my father this day.' I then put my hand in my cloak and wiped my face with a charm given me by my dad. It was my father who bequeathed me that power. I wiped my face with it and could see properly once more.

'The ladybird beetle does not suffer from sight impairment,' [I chanted incantation]. I wiped my face, got back my vision and saw the animal again. I went after it, *my gun spoke* and the animal fell. When I got to it, I clipped its ears and tail and took them home to our fathers in the profession to inform them that I had killed the animal that had eluded us for a long time. But when we returned to the animal, we found it standing. Those who went with me first fled. But I told them, 'Why run? Fire another shot at it.' We tried to shoot but the gun failed. When the gun failed, I untied a charm-belt from my waist and *gave it to the animal.*

Adédùntán: You flogged the animal with it?

Yáwóọrẹ́:   Yes, I flogged the animal with it and it fell. Then we cut it up, took the meat home, and shared it out to whoever wanted to eat.

Now, after we spread and pegged its [the animal's] skin outside to dry, I embarked on another expedition. When I returned, the children reported that a woman came to ask for me, and she had been informed that I was not at home. The woman came back the next day.

'Hello, hunter,' she greeted.

'Hello, old one,' I responded.

'I know you killed a deer. But you did because *we* wanted you to. Now why do you show off with its skin? Why did you spread it out, pegged to the ground outside? You sure want to show the whole world that you it was that killed the animal. Were you the one who actually killed the animal or *we* gave it to you? Don't you know spreading out the hide in the open that way is exposing *our* clothing to the mundane world?'

'Old one, it was Ògún that killed it.'

'Not Ògún, we allowed you to kill it.'

'I am sorry, old one. I did not know that it [the skin] is your cloth.'

I went later to report the matter to our head of hunters, Ọlaifa Adigun. The old man said the woman had come to him the previous day, requesting to see me. He then asked me to go at once and remove the skin from the open. I obeyed him and went home to remove the skin.

Appendix F

The narrative of Kòbọmọjẹ́ Àlàdé[6]

Kòbọmọjẹ́: Ní ọdún díẹ̀ sẹ́yìn, àwọn igbó kan wà tí a jọ má ń dẹ l'ọsàán àt'àwọn èèyàn a wa: àwọn igbò bíí Odò Ògùn, Odò Ọbà, àti igbó ọnà Ìkẹ̀rẹ̀. Àwọn tí a jọ ma ń d'ẹgbẹ́ ni Bàbá Fàbi ní Òkúta Pèmọ́ - ó ti kú níìsìín, k'Ọlọ́un f'ọrun kẹ́ ẹ; wọ́n tún ń pe ọmọ náà ní Kẹ́hìndé Fàbi – òhun náà ti kú, k'Ọlọ́un ọ́ f'ọrun kẹ́ ẹ. Wọ́n ń pe ẹnìkan ní Bàbá Olóògùn, n'Íbùdó Èkaàrún, a jọ ń dẹ'gbẹ́ ni. Wọ́n ń pe bàbá kan ní Bàbá Ayọ̀, a jọ ń dẹ'gbẹ́ ni, àti Bọ́lájí. A ti jọ ma ń dẹ Òkè Ẹbẹdí yìí tipẹ́tipẹ́, lọsàán. Mọ wá rí i pé ẹran pọ̀ ní òkè yí débii pé b'ééyàn bá dẹ'bẹ̀ lálẹ́, nkan ọ́ s'ẹnuu're. Sùgbọ́n ń'gbà a mọ sọ fún àwọn kan, wọ́n ní kí n má lọ l'álẹ́. Mo ní kíni ń bẹ ń'bẹ̀, wọ́n sáà ní kí n má lọ l'álẹ́. N ò sì jẹ́ kí àwọn tí a jọ máa ń dẹ'gbẹ́ ọ́ gbọ́ sí ọrọ̀ yí; àwọn t'áa jọ ń rìn ni mo sọ fún.

Mo kí Olóyè Pọ́ríkú, ó kú àtìlẹyìn mi; tor'àwọn tí mọ gb'ẹmìí lé tí mo fi ń rọ́ lu'núu'jù náà nùun.

Mọ bá tan'ná mọ́rí, mọ bá gun orí ònkóò lọ. Orí Òkè Ẹbẹdí yẹn, yíó fẹ́ẹ̀ tó máìlì márùn-ún, bí òkè hun se gùn tó. Mo rìn títí, mi ò rí ǹkankan. Mọ wáá padà, mọ já firîí lọ sí ìsàlẹ̀ ònkóò hun. Ń'gbàa mo dé'sàlẹ̀, mọ r'ọ̀yà kan, mo yìnbọn lu ọ̀yà hun, sùgbọ́n síbẹ̀síbẹ̀ n ọ̀ pa á. Bí mo se wá ń lọ, mo r'ójú u kiní kan lọ́ọ̀ọ́kán t'ó la gíláàsì. Mo rí i pé ọnà a rẹ̀ jìnà sí mi, mọ bá gbé'ná padà kúrò lójú u rẹ̀, mọ s'ọ̀dọ̀ ọ rẹ̀ d'òòkùn pé kí n lè súnmọ́ ọ dáadáa, kí n fún'gi ń'dìì, k'ígi ó lè gbin. Mo súnmọ́ ọ. Pípadà tí mo ní kí n padà wo ojú ẹran hun, mo tún rí'kan ní ẹgbẹ́ ọ̀dọ̀ mi. Mọ wá ń wò ó wípé èwo ni nwá yìnbọn sí. Sùgbọ́n kí n má wí, kí n má fọ̀, ńse ni mọ ń gbọ́ sawọro àwọn à, àjà ti ńdún, tí ń se 'Worrrrororo!'

Adédùntán: Ààjà kẹ̀?

Kòbọmọjẹ́: Hẹn. N ǹ gbọdọ̀ purọ́; ọdẹ n'ìran àwọn baba à mi. Ọmọ Oròówùsì n'Íbàdàn ni mò ń se. Ọmọ Àpàtí-Àpàtí Ọlọ́rọ̀, ọmọ Lásúdẹ. N'ílù ù'Bàdàn, ọdẹ ni baba à mi. Wọ́n sì l'óókọ. Mọ bá ká'wọ́kò; ń'gbà mo rí i pé sawọro àwọn kinní 'ìí ọ́ mà bò mí mọ́lẹ̀ ẹ. Nlọ́ jẹ́ nkọ́ dúpẹ́ lọ́wọ́ ọ'rú àwọn Olóyè Pọ́ríkú, àt'àwọn baba à mí náà. Mọ bá rìn'ẹ́yìn, pé k'ójú ọ́ má r'íbi . . .

Adédùntán: Ẹ̀ẹ̀ lè maa sálọ?

Kòbọmọjẹ́: Wọ́n ní 'Sánbẹ sùn, f'apó rọrí, ìwà ọmo kíí m'ọmọ ọ́ s'òkígbẹ?' Emi gaan tí mo pilẹ̀ g'òkè Ẹbẹdí lọ, ọrọ̀ eré kọ́. Ń'bo n mọ fẹ́ sálọ? Mọ sá se b'ọkùnrin seé se. Mo kú'ò l'égbẹ̀ẹ̀ ọ̀dọ̀ ọ wọn.

Adédùntán: Iná ti kú?

Kòbọmọjé: Iná ti kú. Mọ bá dú'ó s'égbẹẹ̀ ẹ'gi kan, mo tún'ná mi se. Mọ sá ri i pé mọ padà kú'ò ní sáìdì ọ̀nàa'bi saworo ti ń dún yẹn.

Adédùntán: Àwọn ẹran t'ẹ́ẹ r'ójú wọn ńkọ́?

Kòbọmọjé: Nǹ r'ójú ẹran mọ́. Saworo l'óku tí mọ̀ ńgbọ́.

Adédùntán: Ìlù saworo?

Kòbọmọjé: Ìlù u saworo 'Woroworoworo! Korrorrorro! Jìjìjìjìjìjì!' Mọ bá tún'náà mi se. Sé'bẹ̀rù ejò èé jẹ́ á t'ejò mọ́lẹ̀. Mọ bá bọ́ s'égbẹẹ̀ kejì, mọ bà da fìrì hun padà lọ sí ọ̀nà Ọjà Ẹbẹdí, torí ọ̀nà kan ń bẹ tọ́ já sínú Ọjà Ẹbẹdí gaangan. Ńgbàa mọ sa dé fìrì hun nísàlẹ̀, mọ padà wá ń wo orí ọ̀nkóò yẹn lókè. Bẹ́ẹ̀ni mo tún rí iná méjèèjì hun bí ìgbà tí èèyàn ń sìn-ììyàn á bọ̀.

Adédùntán: Wọ́n tún ń bọ̀ wá s'ọ́dọ̀ ọ yín?

Kòbọmọjé: Wọ́n tún ńbọ̀.

Adédùntán: Haà!

Kòbọmọjé: Ọ́ dáa náà, kò burú.' Wọ́n ní 'Mọ̀jà-mọ̀sá n ni èé p'akíkanjú l'ògun. Akínkanjú tọ́ bá mọ̀jà tí ọ̀ sá, irú u wọn ọ b'ógun u'bòmíì lọ ni.' Ọ̀nàà mí jìn.

Adédùntán: Lát'Ìbàdàn.

Kòbọmọjé: Lát'Ìbàdàn. Àá ti ígbọ́ p'áàjà wá gbé mi lọ.

Adédùntán: Àwọn ǹkan wo lẹ rí ojú wọn yẹn‾

Kòbọmọjé: Pupa l'ojú u wọn l'ójúu'náa ranmáranmà mi. Ńgbàa'lẹ̀ mọ́, mọ wáá lọ bá kan lára àwọn t'áajọ ma ń dẹ'gbẹ́; wọ́n ńpe eléyùùun ní Bàbá Ayọ̀. Mọ wá sọ fún u pé 'Mọ mà dẹ̀'gbẹ́ lọ sí Òkè Ẹbẹdí lánàáà.' Kò ti'ẹ̀ tíì jẹ́ n s'àlàyé t'ó fi sọ pé 'Kílọ lọ̀ọ́ se ń'bẹ̀?' Ó ní láyéláyé kí n má de'bẹ̀ mọ́ o; t'ọ́ bá jẹ́ pé mọ sọ f'óhun kí n tóó lọ, òhun 'ò níí jẹ́ n lọ, torí ọ̀rẹ́ẹ̀ hun kan, àt'ìbọn, àt'àdá, àti gbérí i rẹ̀, ibẹ̀ lọ wà di b'áa se ń sọ̀rọ̀ yí. Àwọn kinní hun, ńgbà tí wọ́n jọọ wọ̀yáà'jà, ọpẹ́lọpẹ́ Ọlọ́un àt'ọpẹ́lọpẹ́ ẹ pé wọ́n bí i wọ́n kọ́ ọ l'ógbọ́n n l'ó jẹ́ ọ padà láàyè. Ó ní ki n má dé'bẹ̀ mọ́ o. Tọ̀ọ̀, àt'ìgbà náà, tí mo fi á padà wá sí ibii wọ́n ti bí mi ní ọmọ, n ọ̀ dẹ̀'gbẹ́ ní Òkè Ẹbẹdí mọ́ o, ibòmíì ni mọ̀ ń dẹ o.

Adédùntán: Ẹ̀ẹ de'bẹ̀ mọ́ lóòótọ́?

Kòbọmọjé: N ọ̀ d'ebẹ̀ mọ́ o, n ọ̀ gbọdọ̀ purọ̀ níwájú Ògún o. N ò dé'bẹ́ mọ́ o, ń'gbà Ọlọ́un ti kó mi yọ t'áàjà ò rù mi lọ. Tọr'ẹni à àjà bá gbé lọ, tí ọ̀ bá pẹ́ẹ́'pọ̀ ní ọ́ l'ọdùn méje, ataare nìkan náà ní ó sì máa jẹ f'ódidi ọdún méje hun.

Adédùntán: Ohun t'ẹ́ẹ r'ójú u rẹ̀ yẹn, ṣ'áàjà ni wọn ń pè é?

Kòbọmọjẹ́: Bí wọn ò ti'ẹ̀ pè é l'áàjà, aà ti mọ̀ p'áàjà ló ni saworo? Ń'gbà èmi ti ń gbọ́ saworo, mo ti mọ̀ p'áàjà ni. Papàá, wọn ìí s'ẹyọ̀ọkan. Bí ọ bá s'ọlá àwọn tí'an fi mí l'émìí balẹ̀ pé kò sí'bi tí mo lè lọ, kò níí s'éwu, wọ́n gbé'lúwa ẹ̀ lọ nùun.

Kòbọmọjẹ́: Some years ago, I used to hunt certain forests in company of my colleagues: the forests include Ògùn River, Ọgbà River and the forest along the road to Ìkẹ̀rẹ̀. I used to hunt in company of Bàbá Fàbi of Òkúta Pẹ̀mọ́ [a place in Isẹyin] who is now dead – may God rest him; there was another colleague called Kẹ́hìndé Fàbi who is also dead now – may God rest him; there was also a man called Bàbá Olóògùn at Ibùdó Èkaàrún, and a man called Bàbá Ayọ̀, and another called Bọ́lájí. We had been hunting together on Ẹbẹdí Heights for a long time, always during the day. I later reasoned that since our daytime expeditions to the mountain were always very successful, a night hunt would yield even a better result. However, when I suggested this to some fellows, they warned me not to go in the night. I asked them for their reasons; they simply maintained that I should not go in the night. However, I did not let in fellow hunters on the matter; I spoke only with non-hunter friends.

I acknowledge Chief Pọ́ríkú for his support and protection; for he is one of those I rely upon in order to confront the forest.

So, I put on my headlight and climbed the mountain. Ẹbẹdí is about five miles from base to the top. I hunted for a long time without sighting any animal. I then started to descend back to the base. When I got to the base, I saw a grass-cutter, fired at it, but failed to hit it. As I continued on my way, I noticed a pair of eyes reflecting my light. As they were far away, I turned the light away from them, casting darkness upon the place so that I could move close to the animal unnoticed before I would *pinch the gun and make it thunder*. I moved closer and noticed that there was another reflecting pair of eyes close to me. As I tried to decide on which of the animals to fire at, I started hearing the bells of the *àànjà* spirits jangling stridently.

Adédùntán: *Àànjà?*

Kòbọmọjẹ́: Yes, I tell no lie; hunting runs in my paternal line. I am of the Oròówùsì family in Ibadan, *a descendant of Àpàtí-Àpàtí Ọlọ́rọ̀, the child of Lásúdẹ*. In the city of Ibadan, my father was a well-known hunter, and very reputable too.

So, I retracted when I saw that I was being overwhelmed by their bells. That is why I acknowledged the likes of Chief Pọ́ríkú, and all my fathers. I then retreated, because in order to avoid disaster . . .

Adédùntán:	Why not flee?
Kọ̀bọmọjẹ́:	There is a proverb: *'The restless man who courts trouble, should he not go to bed in his battle gear?'* I knew already that my nocturnal expedition to Ẹbẹdi was no child's play. So, where do I flee to?
	So, I acted like a real man; I retreated from the spot.
Adédùntán:	Has your light gone out?
Kọ̀bọmọjẹ́:	The light was out. I then moved close to a tree and rekindled my light. I made sure I had cleared out of the way of the jingling bells.
Adédùntán:	Bells?
Kọ̀bọmọjẹ́:	Yes, bells; jangling very loud. I then rekindled my light. You know, *the fear of the venom does not allow you to trample upon the snake*. I moved on to the other side, going downhill towards the path that led to Ẹbẹdí market. When I arrived at the base, I looked uphill and saw those glittering eyes coming as if towards me.
Adédùntán:	Coming towards you?
Kọ̀bọmọjẹ́:	Yes, coming.
Adédùntán:	What?
Kọ̀bọmọjẹ́:	'It's all right,' I said. There is a proverb: *'A warrior who has learnt to retreat as much as he has learnt to advance does not die in battle. All advance and no retreat make the warrior a captive.'* My real home is far away, to which I must return.
Adédùntán:	All the way from Ibadan.
Kọ̀bọmọjẹ́:	From Ibadan. To be captured by the whirlwind would have been unfortunate.
Adédùntán:	Who/What were the owners of those eyes you saw?
Kọ̀bọmọjẹ́:	Those eyes were red in the reflection of my light. At daybreak, I went and reported to a fellow hunter named Baba Ayo. When I told him 'I hunted the Ẹbẹdi Heights last night,' he was immediately alarmed.
	'What on earth were you looking for in that place?' He advised me never to go there again. He said if I had informed him before going, he would have prevailed on me not to go. He said a friend of his once fled that mountain leaving behind his gun, machete and

cloak. But for God and the powers he had been taught, he would not have returned alive. He advised me never to go there anymore.

From that time till I returned to my place of birth, I no longer hunted on Ẹbẹdi; I was hunting elsewhere.

Adédùntán: You actually stopped hunting there?

Kọ̀bọmọjẹ́: Let me not lie to you, for Ogun sees me. I stopped going to hunt in that place. I stopped going, since God had saved me from being taken away by the whirlwind. Whoever is taken away by aaja, the whirlwind, mind you, is kept away for, at least, seven years . . . And such a person would be fed on a sole diet of alligator pepper those seven years.

Adédùntán: Those eyes you saw, did you confirm they belonged to the *à:àjà*?

Kọ̀bọmọjẹ́: I did not have to confirm. Who does not know that *à:àjà* comes in jingles? I knew already by the jingles those were the *à:àjà* spirits. They were in fact more than one. If not for the assurance I had been given that wherever I went, no evil would befall me, I would have ended up taken away by the wind.

Notes

1. Personal interaction, 07/05/2006.

2. Personal interaction, 22/04/2006.

3. Personal interaction, 16/12/2006.

4. Personal interaction, 11/02/2007.

5. Personal interaction, 14/08/2005.

6. Personal interaction, 07/10/2007.

References

Abimbọla, W. 1969a. *Ìjìnlẹ ohùn ẹnu Ifá.* Apá Kejì. Ibadan: Oxford University Press.

_____. 1969b. Yoruba oral literature. Unpublished paper presented at Weekend Seminar on Yoruba Language and Literature. Institute of African Studies, Ife.

_____. 1976. *Ifá: An exposition of Ifá literary corpus.* Ibadan: Oxford University Press.

_____. 1986. An appraisal of African systems of thought. In *The arts and civilization of black and African peoples*, eds. J.O. Okpaku, A.E. Opubor and B.O. Oloruntimehin. Volume 2. 10 volumes. Lagos: CBAAC, 10–29.

Adedeji, J.A. 1981. Alarinjo: The traditional Yoruba traveling theatre. In *Drama and theatre in Nigeria: A critical sourcebook*, ed. Y. Ogunbiyi. Lagos: Nigeria Magazine.

Adeduntan, K.A. 2003. On tradition and innovation: Praise and abuse in the *ìjálá* of Àlàbí Ògúndépò. M.A. project. Department of English. University of Ibadan, viii and 165.

_____. 2008. Calling *àjẹ́* witch in order to hang her: Patriarchal definition and redefinition of female power. In *Global African spirituality, social capital and self-reliance in Africa*, eds. T. Babawale and A. Alao. Lagos: Malthouse, 182–194.

Adepegba, C.O. 2008. Historicity of Yoruba religious tradition. In *The contexts of non-linear history: Essays in honour of Tekena Tamuno*, eds. D. Layiwola, O. Albert and B. Muller. Ibadan: Sefer, 64–89.

Agbájé, B. 1989. *Iṣẹ́ ọdẹ igbó.* In *Iṣẹ́ ìsẹ̀nbáyé*, ed. T.M. Ilésanmí. Ile-Ifẹ: Ọbafẹmi Awọlọwọ University Press, 94–108.

Àjùwọn, B. 1980. The preservation of Yoruba tradition through hunters' funeral dirges. *Africa: Journal of International African Institute* 50(1): 66–72.

_____. 1981. *Ìrèmọ̀jé – eré ìṣípà ọdẹ.* Ibadan: University Press.

_____. 1982. *Funeral dirges of Yoruba hunters*. New York, London and Lagos: Nok.

Anonymous. n.d. Hunter-gatherers. *BookRags*. www.bookrags.com/research/hunter-gatherers-ansc-03 (retrieved 17 December 2005).

Anozie, S.O. 1981. *Structural models and African poetics: Towards a pragmatic theory of literature*. London, Boston and Henley: Routledge and Kegan Paul.

Appiah, A. 1981. Structuralist criticism and African fiction: An analytic critique. *Black American Literature Forum* 15(4): 165–174.

_____. 1992. Spiritual realism. *The Nation*. Aug 3-10: 146–148.

Apter, A. 1992. *Black critics and kings*. New York: University of Chicago Press.

Awoonor, K. 1975. *The breast of the earth: A survey of the history, culture and literature of Africa south of the Sahara*. New York: Anchor and Doubleday.

Babalola, S.A. 1966. *The content and form of Yoruba Ìjálá*. London: Oxford University Press.

Bakhtin, M.M. 1981. *The dialogic imagination*. M. Holquist. Trans. Austin: Texas University Press.

Bamgbose, A. 1974. *The novels of D.O. Fagunwa*. Benin City: Ethiope.

Barber, K. 1991. *I could speak until tomorrow: Oríkì, women and the past in a Yoruba town*. Edinburgh: Edinburgh University Press.

Barthes, R. 1996. Introduction to the structural analysis of narratives. In *Narratology: An introduction*, eds. S. Onega and J.A.C. Landa. London and New York: Longman, 45–60.

Bascom, W. 1965. The forms of folklore: Prose narratives. *Journal of American Folklore* 78(307): 3–20.

_____. 1973. Folklore, verbal art, and culture. *Journal of American Folkore* 86(342): 374–381.

Basset, T.J. 2003. Dangerous pursuits: Hunter association (donzo ton) and national politics in Cote d'Ivoire. *Africa: Journal of the International African Institute* 73(1): 1–30.

Bauman, R. 1973. Folklore, verbal art, and culture. *Journal of American Folklore* 86(342): 374–381.

Bauman, R. and Sherzer, J. 1975. The ethnography of speaking. *Annual Review of Anthropology* 4: 95–119.

Bewaji, J.A.I. 1999. Olodumare: God in Yoruba belief and the theistic problem of evil. *African Studies Quarterly* 2.1. http://web.africa.ufl.edu/asq/v2/3 (retrieved 17 December 2003).

Bhabha, H.K. 1994. *The location of culture*. London and New York: Routledge.

Brecht, B. 1993. The radio as an apparatus of communication. *Semiotext(e)* 6: 15–17.

Bremond, C. 1996.The logic of narrative possibilities. In *Narratology: An introduction*, eds. S. Onega and J.A.C. Landa, London and New York: Longman, 61–75.

Chinweizu, J.O. and Madubuike, L. 1980. *Toward the decolonization of African literature*. Enugu: Fourth Dimension Press.

Cooper, B. 1998. *Magical realism in West African fiction: Seeing with a third eye*. London and New York: Routledge.

Drewal, M.T. 1991. The state of research on performance in Africa. *African Studies Review* 34(3): 1–64.

Echeruo, M.J.C. 1973. The dramatic limits of Igbo ritual. *Research in African Literatures* 4(1): 21–31.

Fagunwa, D.O. 1949. *Igbó Olódùmarè*. London: Nelson.

_____. 1950a. *Ìrèké Oníbùdó*. Lagos: Nelson.

_____. 1950b. *Ogbójú ọdẹ nínú Igbó Irúnmalẹ̀*. Lagos: Nelson.

_____. 1954. *Ìrìnkèrindò nínú Igbó Elégbèje*. Edinburgh: Nelson.

_____. 1961. *Àdììtú Olódùmarè*. Lagos: Nelson.

Finnegan, R. 1970. *Oral literature in Africa*. Oxford: Clarendon Press.

Gates, Jr. H.L. 1983. The 'blackness of blackness': A critique of the sign and the signifying monkey. *Critical Inquiry* 9.4: 685–723.

Gbadegesin, S. 1998. Eniyan: The Yoruba concept of person. In *The African philosophy reader*, eds. P.H. Coetzee and A.P.J. Roux. New York: Columbia University Press, 149–168.

Goldstein, K.S. 1964. *A guide for fieldworkers in folklore*. Hatboro and London: Folklore Associates and Herbert Jenkins.

Hemminger, B. 2001. The way of the spirit. *Research in African Literatures* 32(1): 66–82.

Herskovits, M.J. and F.S. Herskovits. 1958. *Dahomean narrative: A cross-cultural analysis*. Evanston: Northwestern University Press.

Hill, K. 1982. Hunting and human evolution. *Journal of Human Evolution* 11: 521–544.

Idowu, E.B. 1962. *Olodumare: God in Yoruba belief*. London: Longman.

_____. 1973. *African traditional religion: A definition*. Ibadan: Fountain.

Inoue, T. 2001. Hunting as a symbol of cultural tradition: The cultural meaning of subsistence activities in Gwich'in Athabascan society of northern Alaska. *Senri Ethnological Studies* 56: 89–104.

Isola, A. 1976. The place of Iba in Yoruba oral poetry. Unpublished paper presented at the 12th West African Languages Congress, Ife.

Izevbaye, D. 1993. The fired image: Literary beginnings from cultural ends. In *Essays in honour of a Nigerian actor-dramatist*, ed. D. Adelugba. Ibadan: Endtime, 118–134.

_____. 1995. Fagunwa's brave spirit: A study of the contexts of a literary reputation. In *Language in Nigeria: Essays in honour of Ayo Bamgbose*, ed. K. Owolabi. Ibadan: Group Publishers, 250–275.

Jackson, B. 1988. What people like us are saying when we say we're saying the truth. *Journal of American Folklore* 101(401): 276–292.

Jahn, J. 1961. *Muntu: An outline of the new African culture*. New York: Groove Press.

Kagame, A. 1956. *La philosophie Bantu-Rwandaise de l'être*. Brussels: Académie Royale des Sciences Coloniales.

Layiwola, D. 1987. Womanism in Nigerian folklore and drama. *African Notes* 11(1): 27–33.

_____. 1991. Establishing liminal categories in African ceremonial dances. *African Notes* 15(1&2): 19–27.

_____. 1993. Aspects of theatrical circularity in Wale Ogunyemi's dramaturgy. In *Essays in honour of a Nigerian actor-dramatist*, ed. D. Adelugba. Ibadan: Endtime, 52–61.

Leach, M. 2000. New shapes to shift: War, parks and the hunting person in modern West Africa. *The Journal of the Royal Anthropological Institute* 6(4): 577–595.

Levi-Strauss, C. 1998. The structural study of myth. In *Literary theory: An anthology*, eds. J. Rivkin and M. Ryan. Malden, MA and Oxford: Blackwell, 101–115.

Lewis, P. 1981. *Radio drama*. New York and London: Longman.

Lindfors, B. 1973. *Folklore in Nigerian literature*. New York: Africana.

_____. 1999. *The blind men and the elephant and other essays in biographical criticism*. Trenton and Asmara: Africa World Press.

Malinowski, B. 1922, 1948. *Argonauts of the Western Pacific*. London: Routledge.

_____. 1998. Myth in primitive psychology. In *The myth and ritual theory*, ed. R.A. Segal. Malden, MA: Blackwell, 38–57.

Mbiti, J.S. 1970. *African religions and philosophy*. New York: Doubleday.

_____. 1975. *Introduction to African religion*. London: Heinemann.

Motz, M. 1998. The practice of belief. *Journal of American Folklore* 111(441): 339–355.

Mudimbe, V.Y. 1988. *The invention of Africa: Gnosis, philosophy, and the order of knowledge*. Indianapolis and London: Indiana University Press and James Currey.

Na'Allah, A. 1997. Interpretation of African orature: Oral specificity and literary analysis. *Alif: Journal of Comparative Poetics* 17: 125–142.

Ndibe, O. 2000. *Arrows of rain.* Essex: Heinemann.

Ogunsina, J.A. 1987. The sociology of the Yòrúbà novel: A study of Isaac Thomas, D.O. Fágúnwà and Ọládẹ̀jọ Òkédìjí. PhD thesis, University of Ibadan.

Oha, O. 1998. All things wise and wonderful: Nnamdi Azikiwe in Igbo living myths. In *African culture and mythology*, eds. E. Ifie and D. Adelugba. Ibadan: Endtime, 279–289.

Okebalama, C.N. 1991. The hunter in Ubakala Igbo Life. *African Languages and Culture* 4(2): 177–187.

Okpewho, I. 1979. *The epic in Africa: Towards a poetics of the oral performance.* New York: Columbia University Press.

_____. 1983. *Myth in Africa: A study of its aesthetic and cultural relevance.* Cambridge: Cambridge University Press.

Olájùbù, O. 1970. *Àkójọpọ̀ iwì egúngún.* Ibadan: Oxford University Press.

Ọlátúnjí, Ọ. 1972. Ìyẹ̀rẹ̀ Ifá: Yorùbá oracle chant. *African Notes* vii(2): 69–86.

_____. 1984. *Features of Yorùbá oral poetry.* Ibadan: University Press.

Olayemi, V. 1969. *Alọ apagbe nipa awọn ẹranko.* Unpublished paper presented at Weekend Seminar on Yoruba Language and Literature. Institute of African Studies, Ife.

Olomola, I. 1990. Ipade: An extinct aspect of traditional burial rite among Yoruba hunters. *Africana Marburgensia* 23(2): 24–35.

Osundare, N. 1991. Poems for sale. *African Notes* 15(1&2): 63–72.

Oyegoke, L. 1994. 'Sade's testimony': A new genre of autobiography in African folklore. *Research in African Literatures* 25(3): 131–140.

p'Bitek, O. 1973. *Africa's cultural revolution.* Nairobi: MacMillan.

Rabkin, E.S. 1977. *The fantastic in literature.* Princeton, NJ: Princeton University Press.

Raji-Oyelade, A. 1999. Post-proverbials in Yoruba culture: A playful blasphemy. *Research in African Literatures* 30(1): 74–82.

Roscoe, A. 1971. *Mother is gold: A study in West African literature*. London and New York: Cambridge University Press.

Rotimi, O. 1981. The drama in African ritual display. In *Drama and theatre in Nigeria: A critical sourcebook*, ed. Y. Ogunbiyi. Lagos: Nigeria Magazine, 77–80.

Salami, Y.K. 1991. Human personality and immortality in traditional Yoruba cosmology. *Africana Marburgensia* 24(1): 4–15.

Schechner, R. 1993. *The future of ritual: Writings on culture and performance*. London and New York: Routledge.

Sekoni, R. 1990. The narrator, narrative-pattern, and audience experience of narrative performance. In *The oral performance in Africa*, ed. I. Okpewho. Ibadan: Spectrum, 139–159.

Shingler, M. and Wieringa, C. 1998. *On air: Methods and meanings of radio*. London: Arnold.

Smith, R.S. 1988. *Kingdoms of the Yoruba*. Oxford: James Currey.

Soyinka, W. 1963. *A dance of the forest*. London and New York: Oxford University Press.

_____. 1976. *Myth, literature and the African world*. Cambridge: Cambridge University Press.

_____. 2006. *You must set forth at dawn*. Ibadan: Bookcraft.

Tedlock, D. 1977. Toward an oral poetics. *New Literary History* 8(3): 507–519.

Tempels, 1959. *Bantu philosophy*. Paris: Présence Africaine.

Turner, V. 1975. Symbolic studies. *Annual Review of Anthropology* 4: 145–161.

Vansina, J. 1983. Is elegance proof? Structuralism and African history. *History in Africa* 10: 307–348.

White, H. 1996. The value of narrativity in the representation of reality. In *Narratology: An introduction*, ed. S. Onega and J.A.C. Landa. London and New York: Longman, 273–285.

Wiredu, K. 1998. Toward decolonizing African philosophy and religion. *African Studies Quarterly* 1.3. http://web.africa.ufl.edu/asq/v1/4/3.htm (retrieved 17 December 2005).

Yai, O.B. 1999. Tradition and the Yoruba artist. *African Arts* 32(1): 32–34 and 93.

Yankah, K. 1983. To praise or not to praise the king: *Apae* in the context of referential poetry. *Research in African Literatures* 27(2): 381–400.

_____. 1985. Risks in verbal art performance. *Journal of Folklore Research* 22(2/3): 133–153.

_____. 1995. Power and the circuit of formal talk. *Power, marginality and African oral literature*, ed. G. Furniss and L. Gunner. Cambridge, New York and Melbourne: Cambridge University Press, 221–224.

Yemitan, Ọ. 1963. Ìjálá aré ọdẹ. Ibadan: Oxford University Press.

Yerkovich, S. 1983. Conversational genre. In *Handbook of American folklore*, ed. R.M. Dorson. Bloomington: Indiana University Press, 277–281.

Young, S. 2004. Narrative and healing in the hearing of the South African Truth and Reconciliation Commission. *Biography* 27. http://muse.jhu.edu/journals. biography/v027/27.1young.html (retrieved 17 December 2005).

Index

www.ingramcontent.com/pod-product-compliance
Lightning Source LLC
Chambersburg PA
CBHW080555270326
41929CB00019B/3316